13

YEARS OF GOOD LUCK

13 YEARS OF GOOD LUCK
edited by Joe Biel, Dylan Galyan-Wilkerson, and E. Chris Lynch

ISBN 978-1-934620-43-4

This is Microcosm #76100

Second Edition of 3,000 copies - August 12, 2009

Distributed in the booktrade by **AK PRESS**
(510)208-1700 / sales@akpress.org
Available through Baker & Taylor, Ingram, and finer bookstores.

Book design: Ian Lynam | www.ianlynam.com
Cover illustration: Cristy C. Road | www.croadcore.org

MICROCOSM PUBLISHING
222 S Rogers St.
Bloomington, IN 47404-4936
(812)323-7395
www.microcosmpublishing.com

We have other books, zines, t-shirts, patches, stickers, videos, and things available from our catalog and on our website. Send $1 for a catalog.

YEARS OF GOOD LUCK

13 YEARS AGO TODAY I WAS SITTING IN THE ADJOINING ROOM TO MY BEDROOM IN CLEVELAND, OHIO.

Jokingly referring to it as my "office," I put a thrift store desk in there and tacked up cardboard on the ceiling to keep the insulation from falling into boxes of zines and records. As much as I tried to get my friends who were involved in the project to collectivize, they were much more interested in theory than in practice. It didn't take long to figure out that running a distro, particularly one already built on the vision of one strong personality, was still work.

After that house burned down the following year I had an even harder time finding people to come hang out at my mom's house and fill mailorders. It wasn't even the work this time, it was the simple fact that my mom was so sneaky and unpleasant to deal with. So without much help, I would go on tour or disappear for the summer and the mailorders would just sit. Apologies and big thanks to anyone from that era, who put up with late orders and are still around to read this.

Thirteen years later everything has changed. Most notably there's a whole new batch of workers who are more than willing to match my work ethic (possibly even at the potential cost of having to interact with my mom.)

Now instead of dreaming big about dozens of projects but never following through, we publish a new book each month. We're actualizing the dream; publishing zines and books that we believe in while finding better printers to work with who can accommodate the printing techniques we'd like to apply to our books.

Also, I made good on my big teenage dream this past year—a grease-powered cube truck converted to an RV that we use for tour and getting to events. What more can a person ask for?!

The grand plan is a little simplified in this zine though. Each of these reprints represents an in-print project. We had to squeeze a little to make it all fit. With our functional collective decision-making process we seesawed back and forth about this project until we agreed to only reprint things that had appeared in our publications and hadn't been published elsewhere. For books consisting only of reprints we asked the author to draft up some new material for this compilation. We got some new shit from Al Burian, Liz Baillie, Cristy Road, Nate Beaty, and Keith Rosson. Unfortunately, and despite much pleading Adam Gnade was not able to finish his work in progress "Love in The Age of The Terminator".

Looking back on these past 13 years, I am proud of this collection and its goofy title. I kind of feel like it downplays the hard work of my co-workers though. Especially over the last two years, when they had to work harder than ever to pull us out of a $40,000 debt while still raising money for new publishing projects. They did their part, even when I was ready to throw in the towel. Sometimes it takes more than luck.

Which is not to downplay luck, either. Not knowing how to navigate the booktrade allowed us to luck into creating our own system of getting zines and books into record stores, specialty places, and kids' backpacks when the established book industry began to collapse. Also, thanks to us being turned down by every distributor on the planet, we managed to escape the fallout when the distros began going bankrupt and started getting swallowed by Perseus Books.

So as the publishing world continues to fall apart, we're still alive and kicking, and I'm proud to say we put out as much new stuff in the last two years as the 11 years before them. At this rate, you should expect a few surprises and maybe a little evolution from us over the next few years. I can't guarantee we'll last 13 more years, but I can promise we'll do our best in the meantime.

Last year I read a strangely touching article about people who were teenagers when Nirvana broke into the mainstream. Based on the culture they grew up around, a lot of them became career apologists for their own successes. I definitely fell into this trap for a good 10 years and only came to realize how destructive it was after reading the article. We need to abandon our apologizes and embrace our ethics, and we need to do what we do well and use the skills we have to challenge the mainstream's conventions.

Sometimes I talk all idealistic about how the underground is stronger than the mainstream and that book distribution ownership will cease to be a niche hobby investment for rich people and be forced back into the hands of the ingenuitive and passionate publishers and sellers. Other days I just think that stuff is better off ignored and that it's smarter to focus on what you can do well. At least that way you don't get bummed out about what you're up against.

Another confession: This isn't actually our 100th release. There's about a dozen things slated to come out before it that haven't been released yet. Fortunately, we are going to make that up to you because we have tons of rad shit in the works like EDIBLE SECRETS (classified documents about food), the next MY BRAIN HURTS, Joshua Ploeg's IN SEARCH OF THE LOST TASTE, and Matte Resist's HOW & WHY!

My promise for the beginning of our fourteenth year: To be more honest, transparent, and genuine in our goals, ethics, and decision-making process than ever. We're still here because of you and we owe you at least that much.

So thanks for all of your interest and support. It makes it easier to put things in envelopes on hard days and it makes all this feel worthwhile when the future is uncertain.

If you're interested in the history of Microcosm we have a zine called "You Can Work Any 100 Hours That You Want (in your underwear!)" from our 10th anniversary that breaks down the time-line and offers a closer look at where we came from and how we got where we are now.

I think that's it. Get in touch. Let's talk nerdy about zines.

JESSE REKLAW
PO Box 40701
Portland, OR 97240-0401

CRISTY ROAD
PO Box 20229
New York, NY 10009-9991

BILL DANIEL
www.billdaniel.net

SHAWN GRANTON
PO Box 14185
Portland, OR 97293

KYLE BRAVO
1422 Kentucky St.
New Orleans, LA 70117

ETHAN CLARKE
ethansleep@gmail.com

SHELLEY JACKSON
shelleyom@rediffmail.com

DWELLING PORTABLY
juliesummerseatssensibly@
yahoo.com

RALEIGH BRIGGS
letsgiveuptheghost@gmail.com

JOHN ISAACSON
johnisaacson@hotmail.com

CINDY CRABB
PO Box 29
Athens, OH 45701
www.dorisdorisdoris.com

NATE BEATY
1838 N Humboldt Blvd #1A
Chicago, IL 60647
natebeaty.com

MOE BOWSTERN
PO Box 6834
Portland, OR 97228

NICOLE GEORGES
P.O. Box 12763
Portland, OR
www.nicolejgeorges.com

JOE BIEL
P.O. Box 14332
Portland, OR 97293

BILL BROWN
P.O. Box 53832
Lubbock, TX 79453
dreamwhip@gmail.com

BEN SNAKEPIT
PO Box 49447
Austin, TX 78765
bensnakepit@gmail.com

LIZ BAILLIE
www.lizbaillie.com

KEN DAHL
fantods@gmail.com

KEITH ROSSON
2634 SE Morrison
Portland, OR 97214
www.keithrosson.com

DAVE ROCHE
poodrow@hotmail.com

THE URBAN HERMITT
PO Box 20201
Seattle, WA 98102

ANDY CORNELL
403 St. Johns Place #4B
Brooklyn, NY 11238

JOEY TORREY
V-21699 : B10-150L
Mule Creek State Prison
P. O. Box 409040
Lone, California 95640

JOSHUA PLOEG
thetravelingchef@gmail.com

MICHAEL HOERGER &
MIA PARTLOW
ediblesecrets@gmail.com

Only a week left in Portland. Trying not to panic about all the shit we have to do..

Fah funh fuh fahh Cingular blah shmooz

So what do we do but go mobile phone shopping at the mall!

Late..

Artist's rendition of Nate and Soon Bok in LA..

FREE!

We got rid of a ton of stuff in our driveway

.. and stuffed the rest in a 10 ft. UHAUL

I paid some guy $10 to haul away our boxspring — by bike no less!

>URCH< SCREECH! URCH!

Soon Bok drove the Honda for the first time, sans license, from our house to the UHAUL lot.

Uhm...

I was left a booklet on how to hook up the tow dolly

CLANK! CLUNK!

UHAUL 19⁹⁵

I think I hooked everything up right.. It made some awful clunking sound on every bump, but whatever! Off to our 20-hour drive!

This is SUSHI! You want the Sushi?

We stopped in Winston, Oregon at a very out-of-place sushi restaurant.. Just about the last place I'd expect in a podunk Eastern Oregon town. They really pushed the sushi on us... 1) How the hell do you get fresh fish to Winston, and 2) how fresh is it if noone ever orders it??

SUSHI

SOOSHY? AIN'T THAT RAW FEESH??

But! It was better than Subway..

It took me a while to get used to having a mobile phone. Especially being able to check my gmail from anywhere. Quite handy for our roadtrip, tho.

BLEEP!

Like most people I've seen get them, I'm already used to it + find it super useful more often than not..

FDA WARNING! many studies have tried to prove cel phone microwave emissions cause humans harm. But we don't believe it.

Although it did come with an unnerving warning..

$2500 a month?! oh, $2300 without the maid service? You need a credit + background check?

We didn't plan our entry into L.A. very well, and found our-selves battling downtown traffic in a giant UHAUL towing a car.. ACK!

I was used to the open road where everything is sized for semis.

On the 3-day drive down to L.A., we decided against doing one month of corporate housing, opting to try our luck with craigslist.

We'd been relying on Google Maps to find our way, but I still got lost.

We ended up at the Peppertree in NoHo, which looked sketchy as hell.

This ID FISHY!

But it was $50! The owner spent a good five minutes scrutinizing my ID, and refused my Clixel business visa.

Hmmm...

Brown nasty lamp shade

Oldskool tv w/channel knob

ew.

You know, I bet this usually rents by the hour

↑ But! clean sheets!

Bug spray soaked carpet.

TP with red splotch on it.

The oldest known woodcut print in the world is Darani Sutra found inside Seokga Pagoda of Bulguksa Temple, Korea printed before 751 A.D. It predated Japanese Million Pagoda Darani Sutra dated 770 A.D. Chinese printers used wood blocks with carved characters and inked paper in the 8th century. In the 11th century Pi Sheng created early moveable type, allowing for letters to be rearranged. Movable metal type was a development associated with woodblock printing, such as slow engraving. There is a record that Sangjeong-gogeum-yemun (Prescribed Ritual Texts of the Past and Present) was printed with movable type around 1234 A.D.

Johann Gutenberg invented the printing press in 1454, revolutionizing the transmission of information using metal moveable type and an ink made from turpentine, lampblack, and linseed oil. Within 50 years, over 500,000 texts had been printed (almost exclusively religious works). Besides the Bible, one of the first important uses of the Gutenberg press was to print a handbook for the Church called "Malleus Malefactorum," which outlined how to find and expose "witches." It allowed the Church to quickly distribute a kind of uniform code throughout Europe, and is the reason that inquisition questions and procedures across the continent were so quickly disseminated and so similar.

Gutenberg's invention coincided well with the Reformation. Europe, unified as "Christendom" for a millennium, was suddenly ripping apart, and one of the main reasons was that viewpoints opposed to the Vatican were being printed and distributed. Luther's 95 theses, the document that started the conflict, was an early zine – the writing wouldn't have ignited a war if it hadn't been published and passed around.

After 200 years of struggle in England, printers won the right to publish in the 1700s. Beginning around 1760, the Industrial Age created a need for educated workers, which created public schools and wider literacy. Self-publishing was too expensive for most, yet the number of books and pamphlets increased. Ben Franklin self-published as a youth. Samuel Adams, Thomas Payne, and other Americans printed works that helped bring about the American Revolution.

In England, William Blake self-published using etched copper plate engraving. Around 1850, an inexpensive small tabletop printing press, not much more than a toy, introduced "amateur journalism," a popular hobby, especially among boys. Todd Lincoln published on one from the White House, and Lloyd Osborne did a "zine" with contributions from his stepfather, Robert Louis Stevenson. The mimeograph was introduced by Edison circa 1875 and soon became standard office (and church basement) equipment. Dadaists began self-publishing writings and book art in the early 1900s.

And then it happened: In 1929, readers of science-fiction magazines started communicating via mimeographed or spirit-duplicated "fanzines." Pulp novel publishers were inundated with reader mail nitpicking technical details in their stories. So editors began printing letters – complete with full addresses. Fans began writing to each other and forming networks. This led to fanzines about topics such as horror, wrestling, and science fiction. *The Comet,* a science fiction zine composed mostly of articles on science, began publishing in 1930. Other science fiction zines followed, including *Time Traveler* and *Science Fiction*, edited by Jerome Siegel and Joe Schuster, who also created Superman. Many sci-fi zine editors still publish, though most now photocopy or publish online.

Starting in the 1950s, mimeograph technology was used to self-publish literature, including chapbooks and manifestos by the Beats.

American and British punks of the 1970s created the form closest to today's zines, seldom having heard of the original fanzines. Using clip art, they created their own media, using zines to promote independent music and clubs. Cheap and available photocopying made it easier than ever for anyone who could make a flyer to make a zine.

In 1938, Chester Carlson obtained the first patents for the photocopier. In 1937, he developed the process of xerography or "dry copy," a process based on electrostatic electricity. Xerography comes from the Greek term "dry writing." Over twenty companies turned down Carlson's invention, and it took him six years of demonstrating its function before the Battle Development Company took interest and produced his invention in 1944. The Haloid Company negotiated the commercial rights. Haloid became Xerox and introduced the first commercial photocopier in 1958.

In high school, Chester Carlson was a self-publisher himself, using mimeograph. Underground comix artists used the photocopier for self-publishing almost immediately following its introduction. *Rolling Stone* started as a zine. Sergei Kovalev, Tatyana Khodorovich, and Tatyana M. Velikanova self-published *The Chronicle of Current Events* in Russia. Many Russian self-publishers attempted to create a "close circle of like-minded people who spoke their own language, inconceivable to others" under threat of lethal persecution. Even though dissent was not the primary object of many self-publishers, Velikanova was arrested for printing her views, spending four years in a prison camp and five years in exile.

In contrast, a number of people in the USSR self-published purely for dissent, spreading views against nuclear arms and their government's oppression. While not as severe, Americans in the 1960s faced persecution for publishing their work, such as Alan Ginsberg's poem *Howl*. Ginsberg was subjected to a long court trial in which poets and professors were summoned to "prove" that *Howl* was not obscene.

Factsheet Five documented the zine explosion of the 1980s. The original editor, Mike Gunderloy, a pillar of the science fiction fanzine community, popularized the word "zine" and established most of today's "zine ethos" (non-profit, trading, DIY, importance of feedback from readers, etc.) based on his background in the science fiction fanzine tradition.

Technological advances in the 1990s made professional editing and publishing tools accessible to the general public. Mainstream media became interested in zines that had for the most part remained in obscurity for years. They tended to view zines as a novelty rather than as a legitimate form of art or literature. Retail stores began to carry zines as part of their books, comics, or music sections. By the end of the '90s, many who had published popular zines for years stopped publishing, moved into more mainstream creative endeavors, or began to devote their time and creativity to websites.

Today, zines owe creative debts not only to the punk fanzines of the 1970s, but the riot grrl movement of the 1990s. Riot grrl zines were crafted by political feminists, harnessing years of pent-up anger and frustration in the form of cut-and-paste collage and a wicked sense of humor.

The zine explosion of the past two decades had made many people aware of zines. However, the frequent lack of quality jaded some would-be retailers and readers. Digging for the diamond in the rough became more of a challenge and time commitment.

On the other hand, the absence of many long-running zines and the lack of mainstream attention created a fresh, open environment. While mediocre zines were still created, the awareness of what had come before motivated many individuals to create book-art zines and other forms requiring extensive time and effort. Many zine publishers returned to printing methods like silkscreen, letterpress, linoleum cut, and also to hand-stitched bindings.

The use of the Web has created more extensive networks of people working within the same medium. It provides a virtual retail area, increasing reader access to remote locations, and allowing more people to see content than the self-publisher could afford to non-virtually print. Annual conventions aid and regenerate public awareness while strengthening relations among self-publishers.

Today, people who stick to print do so because of its warm, human feel, or distinctive artistic elements. You can use printing techniques that create texture, create pull-out sections, insert envelopes, insert bags with scents, use different kinds of paper, and incorporate other elements that make your zine unique and unable to be reproduced on-screen. Similarly, zines offer an intimate connection in the kinds of information they convey, the vulnerability that the authors often provide, and the simple fact that you can read them in the park, on the bus, or on the toilet.

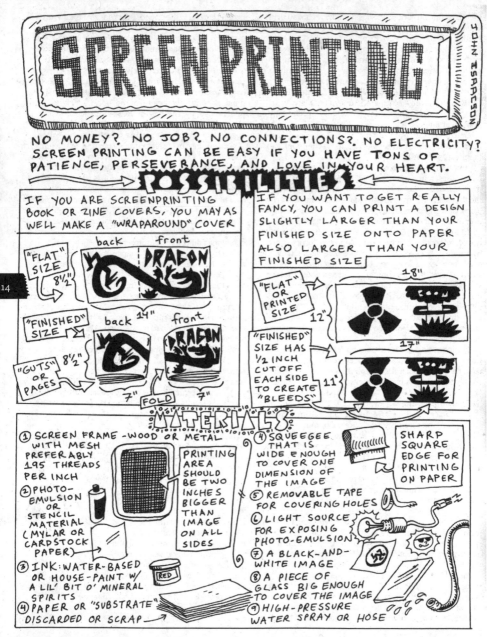

SCREEN PRINTING

JOHN ISAACSON

NO MONEY?. NO JOB?. NO CONNECTIONS?. NO ELECTRICITY?
SCREEN PRINTING CAN BE EASY IF YOU HAVE TONS OF
PATIENCE, PERSEVERANCE, AND LOVE IN YOUR HEART.

POSSIBILITIES

IF YOU ARE SCREENPRINTING BOOK OR ZINE COVERS, YOU MAY AS WELL MAKE A "WRAPAROUND" COVER

"FLAT" SIZE 8½"

back   front
DRAGON

"FINISHED" SIZE

"GUTS" OR PAGES 8½"

back 14" front
DRAGON

7" FOLD 7"

IF YOU WANT TO GET REALLY FANCY, YOU CAN PRINT A DESIGN SLIGHTLY LARGER THAN YOUR FINISHED SIZE ONTO PAPER ALSO LARGER THAN YOUR FINISHED SIZE

"FLAT" OR PRINTED SIZE 12"

18"
BOOM

"FINISHED" SIZE HAS ½ INCH CUT OFF EACH SIDE TO CREATE "BLEEDS" 11"

17"
BOOM

MATERIALS

① SCREEN FRAME -WOOD OR METAL WITH MESH PREFERABLY 195 THREADS PER INCH

② PHOTO-EMULSION OR STENCIL MATERIAL (MYLAR OR CARDSTOCK PAPER)

③ INK: WATER-BASED OR HOUSE-PAINT W/ A LIL' BIT O' MINERAL SPIRITS

④ PAPER OR "SUBSTRATE" DISCARDED OR SCRAP

PRINTING AREA SHOULD BE TWO INCHES BIGGER THAN IMAGE ON ALL SIDES

RED

④ SQUEEGEE THAT IS WIDE ENOUGH TO COVER ONE DIMENSION OF THE IMAGE

⑤ REMOVABLE TAPE FOR COVERING HOLES

⑥ LIGHT SOURCE FOR EXPOSING PHOTO-EMULSION

⑦ A BLACK-AND-WHITE IMAGE

⑧ A PIECE OF GLASS BIG ENOUGH TO COVER THE IMAGE

⑨ HIGH-PRESSURE WATER SPRAY OR HOSE

SHARP SQUARE EDGE FOR PRINTING ON PAPER

14

DESIGNING AN IMAGE

THE SIMPLICITY OF YOUR PRINT IS ALMOST DIRECTLY PROPORTIONAL TO THE NUMBER OF COLORS IN IT.

OVER THROW THE GOVERNMENT TOMORROW PEOPLE'S PARK

1 COLOR

FASHION SHOW

2 COLORS- NON-REGISTERING

BAD DUDES

3- COLORS- TIGHT REGISTRA- TION

EASY → MODERATE → DIFFICULT

IF YOU ARE USING WATER-BASED INKS, YOU CAN CREATE ADDITIONAL COLORS BY OVERLAPPING COLORS

TWO COLOR PRINT

CREATES THREE COLORS

BLUE

YELLOW

GREEN MADE BY OVER-LAPPING YELLOW AND BLUE

15

YOU MUST SEPARATE THE COLORS BY HAND OR DIGITALLY ON A COMPUTER. PRINT OR DRAW EACH COLOR ON A SEPARATE TRANSPARENT SHEET

C A Y

BLUE

R Z

YELLOW

REGISTRATION MARKS HELP TO LINE UP THE COLORS WITH EACH OTHER... ✛ ⊕

EACH IMAGE MUST BE PRINTED OUT IN BLACK IN ORDER TO BLOCK-OUT LIGHT WHEN THE SCREEN IS EXPOSED.

LIGHT
SCREEN
GLASS
IMAGE

PHOTO EMULSION

DESIGNING AN IMAGE WITH NO COLORS THAT TOUCH EACH OTHER WILL SAVE YOU THE STRESS OF TIGHT, EXACT COLOR REGISTRATION

THE CRAZY SADLOLS PLAYING AT THE BOTTOM OF THE SHOE

11/17 8PM $4.00

PRETEND THIS IMAGE IS BLUE

PRETEND THIS TEXT IS RED

VISUALIZE THIS "PAPER" AS A CREAMY OFF-WHITE

REMEMBER YOU CAN USE THE PAPER AS ANOTHER COLORFUL ELEMENT IN YOUR DESIGN.

STENCIL

PRINT

PAPER COLOR

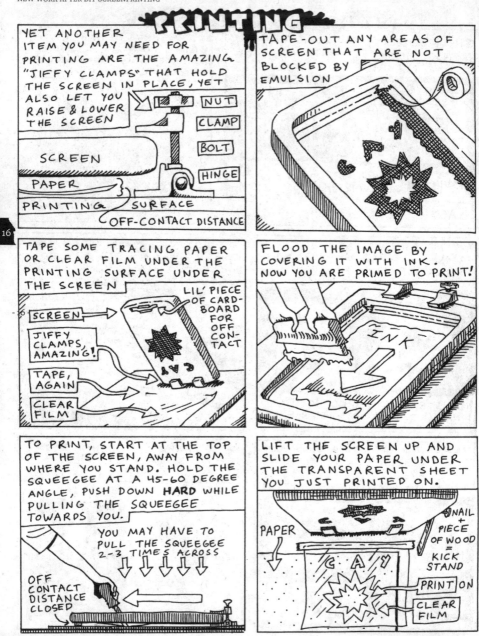

PRINTING

Panel 1:
YET ANOTHER ITEM YOU MAY NEED FOR PRINTING ARE THE AMAZING "JIFFY CLAMPS" THAT HOLD THE SCREEN IN PLACE, YET ALSO LET YOU RAISE & LOWER THE SCREEN

NUT
CLAMP
BOLT
HINGE
SCREEN
PAPER
PRINTING SURFACE
OFF-CONTACT DISTANCE

Panel 2:
TAPE-OUT ANY AREAS OF SCREEN THAT ARE NOT BLOCKED BY EMULSION

Panel 3:
TAPE SOME TRACING PAPER OR CLEAR FILM UNDER THE PRINTING SURFACE UNDER THE SCREEN

LIL' PIECE OF CARDBOARD FOR OFF CONTACT
SCREEN
JIFFY CLAMPS, AMAZING!
TAPE, AGAIN
CLEAR FILM

Panel 4:
FLOOD THE IMAGE BY COVERING IT WITH INK. NOW YOU ARE PRIMED TO PRINT!

INK

Panel 5:
TO PRINT, START AT THE TOP OF THE SCREEN, AWAY FROM WHERE YOU STAND. HOLD THE SQUEEGEE AT A 45-60 DEGREE ANGLE, PUSH DOWN **HARD** WHILE PULLING THE SQUEEGEE TOWARDS YOU.

YOU MAY HAVE TO PULL THE SQUEEGEE 2-3 TIMES ACROSS

OFF CONTACT DISTANCE CLOSED

Panel 6:
LIFT THE SCREEN UP AND SLIDE YOUR PAPER UNDER THE TRANSPARENT SHEET YOU JUST PRINTED ON.

NAIL + PIECE OF WOOD = KICK STAND
PAPER
PRINT ON CLEAR FILM

EXPOSING THE IMAGE

POUR A BEAD OF EMULSION* ON THE SCREEN:

"TEXTURE"

EMULSION

BUCKET

"POURING"

"BEAD"

* MANY TYPES OF EMULSION MUST BE MIXED WITH A SENSITIZER FIRST!

USING A STRAIGHT-EDGE OR PIECE OF CARDBOARD, SCRAPE THE EMULSION EVENLY ON TO THE SCREEN

A THIN COAT WORKS BEST

YOUTH OF TODAY

EMULSION

ALSO WORKS

COAT IN BOTH DIRECTIONS ON BOTH SIDES

LET IT DRY OVERNIGHT IN THE **DARK**. EXPOSING THE SCREEN TO **LIGHT** WILL MAKE THE EMULSION HARDEN AND BECOME WATER PROOF = MAGICAL POWERS

BOTTOM OF SCREEN

DARKNESS

LIL' BLOCKS

SET UP YOUR EXPOSURE SYSTEM. THE VARIABLES ARE WATTAGE, SCREEN SIZE, DISTANCE BETWEEN LIGHT SOURCE AND SCREEN, AND DURATION OF EXPOSURE.

ULTRA VIOLET LIGHT

EXPOSURE TIME ≈ TEN SECONDS

EXPOSURE TIME ≈ TWO MINUTES

250 WATT BULB

SCREEN BOOK

HOT TIP: USE A PIECE OF GLASS TO KEEP IMAGE IN CONTACT WITH THE SCREEN

LIGHT

CAY

BLUE

WET TIP: WASH SCREEN OUT **IMMEDIATELY** AFTER EXPOSURE

WATER SPRAY

EXPOSED EMULSION

CAY

UNEXPOSED EMULSION

17

COMPOST for beginners

Everyone loves composting. It's a fact! Tending a compost heap is the easiest, cheapest, most environmentally sound way to create healthy soil for your garden. If you don't already have a compost pile in your yard or apartment complex, here's how it should go down:

① Grab a trash bag and a bucket. Use the bag(s) to collect stuff like paper scraps, straw, dead leaves, and other dry material. What you'll have is a bag full of carbon-rich substance that will form the base of your compost.

Meanwhile, fill the bucket with nitrogen-rich matter like grass clippings, food scraps, aged manure (see note), and so on. Many of my friends keep a lil' bucket under their sink just for compost fodder. FYI, you can also compost:

- bread products
- egg- and nutshells
- flat beer
- lint
- wood ashes
- junk mail (shredded)

② Find a spot in your yard and, if you wish, build an enclosure for your compost. You could buy one, of course, but it's just as easy to nail some pallets together, or bend some wire mesh into a cylinder. A big pile in a corner of the yard is also fine.

20

③ To build your compost, start with a bed of dry, carbon-y stuff about 6 inches deep. On top of that, spread a 2 inch deep layer of nitrogen material. Then, the icing, as it were: a shovelfull of dirt from your garden. The garden soil will introduce the organisms that will be making your compost.

④ Repeat these three layers until the pile is about three feet tall. This part goes by very quickly if you have some friends and a couple of extra shovels. Try to keep the ratio of dry stuff to moist stuff at around 3:1.

⑤ Water your compost until the whole thing is just damp, but not wet.

whee!

⑥ Over the next couple of months, this pile should get quite warm. This is a good sign, as it signals that decomposition is taking place. If, after a month, it's not warm at all, add some more moist, rotting vegetation. Once or twice a month, turn the compost well using a shovel or pitchfork. Doing so will redistribute the decomposing organisms, which tend to migrate towards the center of the pile. Add more organic material (carbon stuff and nitrogen stuff) as you acquire it.

If it's well-tended, a compost heap should be ready within 6 months. You can tell the heap is ready if it's dark, crumbly, and has a lovely fresh-earth smell.

NOTE: People disagree about whether or not to compost cat and dog poo. Carnivore feces can contain a lot of harmful bacteria that you don't want near edible plants. Because of this, most folks will tell you to keep any and all dog/cat/wolf shit far from your compost. However, some people argue that a very active compost heap can get hot enough to kill pathogens – 160°F, to be exact. So, if you want to compost pet waste, please make sure you've got a real rager of a compost pile going. Otherwise, toss your shit elsewhere.

Choosing the Right Bike!

What kind of riding do you do? Are there a lot of hills where you live? Do you bike a long distance every day? Do you carry a lot of stuff, or move heavy things a lot? Is your bike for recreation or transportation? These questions will help you choose a good (and appropriate) bike for your town and your lifestyle.

CRUISER
(THIS ONE HAS
A GIRL'S FRAME)

Cruiser - this is the single-speed, heavy-duty sit-up-straight style bike. In California we called them beach cruisers; in New Orleans we call them truck bikes. Cruisers have wide tires, wide seats and are often weighted down by fenders, chain guards and wide or tall handle bars. Schwinn made great ones, Murray made decent ones, and Huffy made some pretty crappy ones. New retro cruisers are making a comeback and even come with "distressed" paint to get that old school look that folks love these days. These are great bikes for big baskets and lots of hauling. Not so good for uphill riding. I ride my dog around on mine!

THREE-SPEED
BIKE

Three speed - these were most popular in the 70s and 80s and were made popular by department stores. They are lighter than cruisers, usually have internally geared hubs and dove bars. These are great bikes and it isn't hard to find a good old one in nearly mint condition. Tunes up well and are surprisingly fast, and when the hub goes, it's easily converted to a nice light single speed with a coaster wheel. These are strong and generally faster than cruisers. They'll hold a fair amount of weight too.

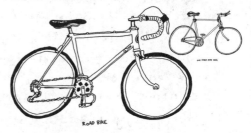

ROAD BIKE

Road bike - light bikes with multiple gears (10-27), drop bars and made, in most cases, with either steel or aluminum. Built for racing, but used by commuters and weekend distance riders. Road bikes can be the fastest, but with the thinner tires and drop bars, they're not for everyone. These are the bikes that are often very easily converted to single speeds for flatter terrain. You can mount a good rack on the back of them for transporting light stuff.

TRACK BIKE

Track bike - These were built for riding on a, um, track. They are light, road style

22

bikes with one gear cog in the front and one in the rear. Unlike single-speeds, which have a freewheel in the back, track bikes have a fixed cog which prevents the bike from coasting, (meaning, if the wheels are turning, so are the cranks, pedaling all the time). . These are popular with bike messengers, and are most easily recognized by the lack of brake levers. They are meant to be light and simple (no derailleurs, no brakes, no cables, no shifters) and almost never having anything extra like racks or baskets-though it has been done.

COMFORT
BIKE

MOUNTAIN BIKE

Mountain bike - mostly straight-framed bikes with larger knobby tires and multiple gears (usually 18-27). They usually have straight handlebars with low stems for a more aggressive ride, often with front and/or rear suspension (shocks). The knobby tires slow you down a bit in the city, but can be switched out for slicks, un-less you ride in dirt or grass or off-road a lot. Suspension complicates baskets and racks.

Cross bike/hybrid - similar looking to mountain bikes, only suited more for commuters. Often with cushier seats, slicker street tires (on narrower 700c wheels), higher handlebars and stems for a more upright position. Some have shocks, or seat post shocks. Hybrids were almost the perfect city commuter bike until most companies switched to only comfort bikes.

Comfort bike - These are pretty new school as far as I can tell. I think I was working at French Quarter Bikes when the big switch happened and most companies left out the hybrid and got these. They are similar also to mountain bikes, usually have wider but slicker tires. They often come with shocks on the front forks and on the seat posts; wide seats too. They usually have very high adjusting handlebars and stems and are actually very comfortable but slower than a hybrid and more complicated for basketing (due to the shocks), which I think is pretty important for a commuter.

BMX BIKE

BMX - short dirt/street/jump/trick bikes, usually with 20 inch wheels and tiny frames. Fun for tricks, but a little difficult for transportation riding. Though Ethan used to know a maniac who couriered on one.

24

CONFLICTS WITH AUTHORITIES

In 1997, the mayor of San Francisco, Willie Brown, was asked by a journalist at a press conference how he planned to control the Critical Mass bike ride. The mayor was quoted in the press as threatening the riders with arrest, along with various belittling of bicyclists. The reaction and extensive press coverage grew into a confrontation at the July 25, 1997 ride. The local newspapers had published a route, although many riders were hesitant about—or flatly against—cooperation with it. On Friday the mayor addressed the crowd at the Embarcadero meeting place but was shouted down. The crowd of approximately 7,000 bicyclists quickly split into many parts, each being chased or monitored by police units, including helicopter monitoring. This resulted in extensive turmoil throughout the downtown area and many arrests and bicycle confiscations.

Police tactics normally default to either attacking the ride and trying to spur a confrontation that they will inevitably win through sheer force and numbers - or they attempt to portray themselves as the protectors, endorsers, - or even sponsors of the ride! On one occasion at a Bay Area ride, the police announced "Welcome to this event!" and greeted people. A newcomer might be led to believe that the police had planned and executed the ride.

It is important not to escalate violence with the police. This is what they want. It makes them appear needed. When the police request the ride to file into a single lane, it is best to comply and file back into both lanes after they disappear. This undermines their tactic of confrontation. After several attempts at controlling the ride, the police normally back off, realizing that they would have to instigate violence or arrest everyone. This causes a shift back to the tactic of acting like public servants to the ride.

NO LIFE
9 A.M. TO 5 P.M.
MON. TO FRI.
BRAIN CLEANING

YO STP or STDs?
CONDOMS FOR OIL TANKERS

NO TICKETS
FREE PARKING

YO HOW LONG IS YOUR COMMUTE?
7 A.M. - 9 A.M.
5 P.M. - 8 P.M.
Save Time, Ride a Bike!

After the US 2004 Republican National Convention coincided with the August 2004 New York City Critical Mass, many court cases resulted regarding the legality of the ride, confronting issues of whether police have the right to arrest cyclists and seize their bicycles, and whether the event needs a permit. In December of 2004, a federal judge threw out New York City's injunction against Critical Mass as a "political event.". On March 23, 2005, the city filed a lawsuit, seeking to prevent TIME'S UP!, a local nonprofit, direct action, environmental group, from promoting or advertising Critical Mass rides. The lawsuit also stated TIME'S UP! and the general public could not participate in riding or gathering at the Critical Mass bike ride, claiming a permit was required. The documentary *Still We Ride* discusses this situation in detail and shows the nature of these bike rides before and after the police took notice.

In September 2005, Critical Mass in London found itself in conflict with public law enforcement when the Metropolitan Police gave out notices announcing a requirement that the organizers of the mass report a route six days before the event. In addition, they stated that the mass

may be restricted in the future, and arrests would result if their orders were not followed. The threat was quickly moderated when politicians and cyclist groups voiced objections. The following ride - on October 2005 - was tremendously well attended, with estimates approaching 1,200 participants. There was a long stop in Parliament Square, part of the Government's exclusion area in the Serious Organised Crime and Police Act 2005. However, this event also led to a particularly slow and cumbersome ride which brought some debate from London cycling groups.

Another consequence of the police notice was that a participant sought a declaration from the High Court of England and Wales that there was no requirement to seek police permission for the Critical Mass rides. After what the judgment describes as a "friendly action" in which the claimant and the police agreed not to seek damages, the Court's ruling on June 27, 2006 agreed that the Critical Mass rides did not fall within section 11 of the Public Order Act 1986 and therefore no notice had to be given.

We Have Lived in Our 18' Diameter Yurt for Eight Years Now

It still has the original canvas (Pyrotone - 50/50 poly/cotton) roof, which we waterproofed by painting with exterior latex house paint (this doesn't work on untreated cotton canvas by the way). We need to replace our 100% cotton walls, and maybe we will this year - otherwise I'll patch the rot spots.

I wouldn't live in any other kind of structure. Even with the paint the yurt is very light. It is round, it uses space much better than a tipi, and it's beautiful.

Last year we were in northern Arizona for six months and lived in a 10' yurt. We used a white parachute over 4 mil plastic for the roof and we _really_ enjoyed the light - especially the light of the stars. It was not a durable arrangement for the high desert sun, and we had to cover it with a blue plastic tarp after three months. Incidentally, we had an outdoor kitchen, so the yurt was primarily sleeping space.   Anne Schein, California, June 1987

Tipis Can Be Comfortable but are Not Very Light

You need an inside lining to keep comfortable in a tipi in really cold weather. The tipi is the only type of tent shelter in which you can have an open fire for winter warmth. But they are large and heavy and need long poles. A tipi is _not_ a backpack tent and _not_ cheap. It is pretty much a two man job to pitch. It's the only type of tent I have not slept in, though I have spent many afternoons in friends' tipis.

There is one best book on the tipi. Try your local library for The Indian Tipi by Reginald & Gladys Laubin, U of Oklahoma Press, Norman, OK 73019. Price $21.95. Ernest Thompson Seton also wrote on tipis. Lyman Barry, NY, March

There is Much Good Camping in Northern California

The river canyons are largely empty and beautiful. I've been mining for gold on the North Fork American between Truckee and Sacramento. Pretty good gold at end of summer. Paul Rinne

My Three Children and I Enjoy Sled-Dog-Team Winters

And camper-backpacker summers. I spent much of my childhood on pack horses in the high Sierras. Joni, Alaska, March

Shelter Systems' New Portable Domes Have Shingled Covers

I've completed work on a new dome - The LightHouse (TM). The 18' diameter size is 9' tall, and has four doors and four clear vinyl triangular windows. It weighs 60 pounds. Packed size is 5'x18"x18". It will sell for $560 but I've a kit complete except for poles and stakes for $390. The kit can be assembed in under five hours.

Because all panels are shingled and clipped (no sewing) it is 100% leak proof and yet breathes. Bob Gillis, Dec

Shelter Systems also has a 12' diameter LightHouse, shown in the picture. 6½' high, weight 38 pounds, packed size 4'x12"x12". Assembled, it sells for $389.

The LightHouse goes up in 30 minutes without tools, according to the info sheet. You simply insert interchangeable poles into connectors spaced evenly over the cover.

The poles are bent slightly when inserted and this tightens
the cover. Once up, the LightHouse is free standing and can
be moved. It comes down in five minutes.
    The sidewalls are of a 5.5 oz polyester canvas, colored
light tan. The translucent skylight above the sidewalls is
constructed of a woven, ripstop, UV resistant film.
A sunshade of silver and black ripstop covers the top of the
dome. The frame is PVC tubing. Lexan clips join the covering
without puncturing or weakening. In tropic weather the sidewalls can be rolled up to provide unsurpassed ventilation -
net sidewalls are an option. Shelter Systems, Box 67, Aptos,
CA 95001 (408)662-2821. Catalog $1.

<u>Domes</u> <u>Or</u> <u>Tunnels</u>? <u>Shingles</u> <u>Or</u> <u>Big</u> <u>Sheet</u>?
    I wonder about shingling. If the overlapping pieces lay
snug together, how do they breathe? If there are gaps between
them, will insects or rain get through? I was told that a
wooden shingled roof must be steep, else it will leak.
    The thought came to me that shingling was invented when
there were only natural materials in small pieces (bundles of
thatch, skins).   Now that fabrics are made long and wide,
the arc or tunnel shape (like the greenhouse plans you sent
previously) or the shed shape (like the tleanto in MP Sept.
1986 p.1, or the Woodland Tent in LLL) seems simpler to make
and a more efficient use of material. Also all the vents,
doors and windows can be on the ends of the shelter under the
overhanging roof, rather than on surfaces that must shed rain.
    On the other hand, with shingling if one piece gets holed
only it needs replacement, rather than the whole cover.
(A patch on plastic doesn't hold up long in our experience.)
Also a dome-shape frame is stronger for the same weight (or
lighter for the same strength) than an arc-shaped or shed-
shaped frame, because the poles brace each other in more
different directions. Bert, Oregon, January
    It's true that large sheeting lends itself to tunnel and
cone shapes. However, I've found that with the same amount of
strength of poles, I achieve more stiffness (i.e. strength)
with domes than with tunnel shapes because of cross bracing
(as you pointed out). Domes also fit into the environment
more pleasingly, some feel. Many people like the looks of
domes better than the tunnel shapes I make. Plus domes
provide more headroom near the walls than do shed or cones.
And domes use shorter poles and are thus more portable.
    Besides allowing creation of dome shapes, shingling
allows use of woven 6' wide material (which is much stronger
than plastic film, though more expensive and not as available
except as blue tarps). Shingling also lends itself to
combining a variety of materials. E.g., the LightHouse has
a top of silver/black to produce shade; upper side walls of
translucent for lighting; clear vinyl windows for visibility;
fabric sidewalls for doors and privacy. The shingling allows
for extensive upper venting without leakage.
    The shingled overlapped edges are pulled tight between
the clips and this creates ridges which make the seams water
tight even on a ridge point. My understanding of "why

shingling must be steep" is because of cracks and nail holes
in the shingles that will leak if not steep enough. With the
LightHouse, the clips used for joining do not puncture the
covering, so no leakage. Bob Gillis, California, February

(Other articles regarding merits of various shapes for
portable dwellings are in MP Sept.1983   , Sept. 1985
and   Sept. 1986   .)

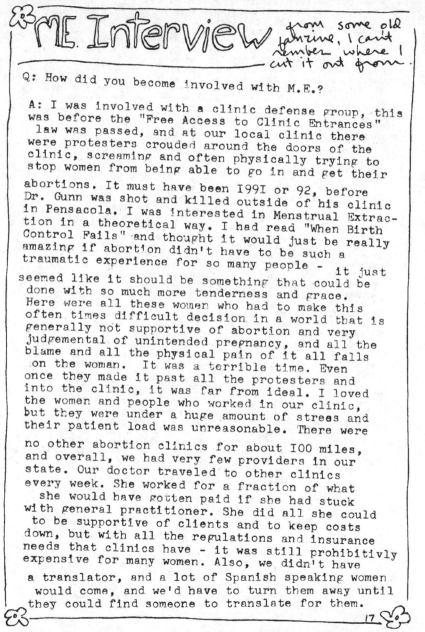

M.E. Interview

from some old fanzine, I can't ember where I cut it out from.

Q: How did you become involved with M.E.?

A: I was involved with a clinic defense group, this was before the "Free Access to Clinic Entrances" law was passed, and at our local clinic there were protesters crouded around the doors of the clinic, screaming and often physically trying to stop women from being able to go in and get their abortions. It must have been 1991 or 92, before Dr. Gunn was shot and killed outside of his clinic in Pensacola. I was interested in Menstrual Extraction in a theoretical way. I had read "When Birth Control Fails" and thought it would just be really amazing if abortion didn't have to be such a traumatic experience for so many people - it just seemed like it should be something that could be done with so much more tenderness and grace. Here were all these women who had to make this often times difficult decision in a world that is generally not supportive of abortion and very judgemental of unintended pregnancy, and all the blame and all the physical pain of it all falls on the woman. It was a terrible time. Even once they made it past all the protesters and into the clinic, it was far from ideal. I loved the women and people who worked in our clinic, but they were under a huge amount of strees and their patient load was unreasonable. There were no other abortion clinics for about 100 miles, and overall, we had very few providers in our state. Our doctor traveled to other clinics every week. She worked for a fraction of what she would have gotten paid if she had stuck with general practitioner. She did all she could to be supportive of clients and to keep costs down, but with all the regulations and insurance needs that clinics have - it was still prohibitivly expensive for many women. Also, we didn't have a translator, and a lot of Spanish speaking women would come, and we'd have to turn them away until they could find someone to translate for them.

28

There were death threats to the clinic workers and
the doctor had to move twice because of pretests
outside her house. She had a daughter in element-
ary school, and the protesters threatened her d
daughter as well. There were bomb scares at the
clinic. I'm sure it was a very stressful
enviornment to be in day after day, and while
I know the doctor and workers wanted to provide
a calm and healing enviornment, they simply weren't
able to.   Quite honestly, it sort of felt like an
assembly line in there sometimes.

Q: So you saw M.E. as an alternative to this?

A: Partially, yes. Not as an alternative exactly,
Clinics are obviously incredably important and
it is essential that we fight against restrictive
abortion laws, that we support our abortion
providers, volunteer at clinids and work toward
creating the clinics of our dreams.

   I'm not at all confident that abortion will
remain legal, so learning M.E. is important
for that reason, but I also think it is important
to create the world we want to live in, and if
I ever have an un wanted pregnancy again, I want
to be able to terminate it amongst friends, with
my partner there, and to have the kinds of support
I need. I want it to be a time when I can reflect
and let go and feel my feelings and not be
judged.

The scope of what we need to do to create a world
where women have full reproductive freedom is
huge - abortion is only a tiny part of it, and
M.E. is a tiner part of it.
   The group I was in didn't start out as an M.E.
group. We had a wide range of interests.

       At first we were mainly educating ourselves
about the feminist movement and political policies,
and we studied anatomy (which made me very uncomfor-
_table.) and we researched about the different
kinds of birth control. There was a stigma about
women's health groups in the radical community at
the time - jokes about us getting together and

dropping our pants, but the reality was, we
didn't even consider doing self exam type stuff
until the group had been going for a long time.
Some of the women were interested in it, but I for
one,   was   not. I had no interest in letting
anyone else see my body, and honestly, didn't
really see the point. What eventually happened,

is we got really interested in herbal abortion,
it really seemed like the solution. Then I got
pregant, and we tried herbs, and it
didn't work. someone else in our group
got pregnant, we tried again, it didn't
work. We got very depressed about it all.
Now, I know people who have had success
with herbs, but I know more people who
haven't. Anyway, that is when we
seriously started to try and learn a
about M.E.

Q: What were your first steps?

A: We started studying anatomy and physiology
much more seriously. We started reading everything
we could get our hands on about ME. We started
learning about whatever we could - sterilization
techniques, std's, what complications can occur
and what do you do about them. We went over
different scenarios.

Q: What kind of scenerios?

A: Emergency scenerios. Like what to do if someone goes in to shock, what to do if there's a
hemorrhage or a perforation. If you're trained
properly, M.E. is very safe, but it is important
to take it seriously andknow how to deal with
emergencies.

We took a CPR class and also practiced counciling
skills. We started to get closer as a group,
dedicating more time to eachother as friends,
outside the group, and addressing more personal
things inside the group - boundry issues, body
issues, abuse, previous abortions, We did
stretches and self-defense warm ups - trying to

become more embodied as a group and stronger, and just to be more relaxed and have some fun. Eventually, we started doing speculum exams and a nurse friend of ours taught us pelvic exams. For awhile it seemed like that was as far as we'd ever get.   It just seemed like how would we ever learn to actually do M.E. or get the last bits of equiptment we hadn't managed to get. We tried to become a little bit more visable as a health group - teaching classes about birth control and fertility awareness, and eventually we found someone who wanted to teach us.

Q: How did you find them?

A: I think if you are in a group long enough, someone will just come and find you.

Q: Can you talk a little about the pro's and cons of M.E.?

A: Abortions can be done much later than M.E.s. Every group is different, but our group didn't do them past 6 weeks from the last menstrual period. We found that after 6 weeks, there was a higher risk of incompletes, and the procedure just took too long. May be if our group had lasted longer, we would have gained more skills and been able to do them later, but it really is designed for early pregnancy, at least that's my opinion. There are a lot of benefits to having it done at a clinic. It is quicker, you can have sedatives, you can use a wider range of defense mechanism to pull you through it.

Q: What do you mean?

A: With M.E. you really have to be present in your body, before, durring and after the procedure, you have to be aware of how you are feeling during the procedure, and be able to communicate what is going on. It is very emotional for many people to experience pain and vulnerability around people who care about them. For many of us, it is a basic survival skill to cut ourselves off from our emotions.

31

COINTELPRO

COINTELPRO is an acronym for the FBI's domestic "counterintelligence programs" to neutralize political dissidents. Although the FBI has always used covert operations, the formal activities of 1956-1971 were broadly targeted against radical political figures such as Martin Luther King and his followers. Its goals are to discredit and undermine activist groups working domestically in the US. Since they believed their aims to be so righteous they would really stop at nothing to accomplish their goals including blackmail, threatening families, and politically lynching people with the media.

The FBI had been wiretapping King for years and planting paid informants inside his organization to gather information. They referred to him as "Zorro", the Spanish word for fox or "The Fake Messiah". In 1968 the FBI increased the surveillance even further as President Johnson feared that King would drive him out of the White House. Bugs were planted at "all present and future addresses" of King under approval from Robert Kennedy. The justification was that he was perceived to be a communist or acting under communist influence. These allegations have never had any supporting evidence. Hoover interpreted the permission to mean that anywhere King stayed or spent extensive amounts of time could be bugged, such as hotel rooms, friends' houses, families' houses, and more. No substantial evidence was ever produced as a result of this or in support of this justification. King spoke out about how the FBI wasn't doing its job to protect him and other blacks in the south. The FBI took that comment personally and a full scale espionage war was on. In the end the wiretaps broke the privacy rights of 5,000-6,000 people.

Cartha DeLoach was the head of COINTELPRO in 1968. At one point FBI agents including Cartha were trying to get in touch with King to meet with him. His office was particularly busy at this time and their calls were not returned. Being ignored tarnished the FBI's image of King even more than being berated and criticized. Cartha talked about "removing" King and called him "the fake messiah".

One of Hoover's favorite methods was blackmail and the best way for a group of conservative old white religious men to embarrass or discredit someone was with charges of sexual promiscuity or adultery. Often times bugged tapes were doctored or improved to make a stronger blackmail case. It got to the point where they would blackmail King and then send

him anonymous letters trying to persuade him to commit suicide. Other letters to his wife included "improved" tapes of King in supposed sexual situations with other women and then they attempted to persuade her to leave him.

COINTELPRO operatives discredited King by infiltrating black movements and turning marches and protests violent. On King's visit to Memphis on March 28, on a march in support of the sanitation strike, the march was turned violent by undercover police and FBI agents posing as members of a militant group called "The Invaders". The police did nothing to stop the violence and property destruction until the march came through at which point they violently attacked the protestors.

"The October Surprise"

Immediately after the U.S. Embassy was stormed by Iranian students, President Carter's popularity surged as Americans rallied behind their president. However, as the hostage crisis dragged on, it began to affect Carter's image. Carter became more desperate to end the crisis. He approved a rescue mission that ended in dismal failure when two helicopters filled with U.S. Army Special Forces teams crashed in the desert and killed everyone aboard. Carter took responsibility for the incident, which left him with an aura of helplessness and weakness.

1980 was an election year in the United States, a fact of which the Iranians were well aware. The U.S. was beginning to go through a recession that was due in part to an increase in oil prices, driven by the instability in Iran. Carter's approval ratings in the U.S. seemed to plummet with each passing day. One of the primary reasons that the Iranians continued to hold the U.S. hostages was specifically because the hostage crisis was embarrassing the U.S. president.

Another reason for the length of the hostage crisis, it has been alleged, was that the Committee to Elect Ronald Reagan prolonged the crisis through secret deals with the Iranians - aimed at further embarrassing Carter before Election Day, 1980.

The Reagan-Bush Campaign was helped immensely by the ongoing hostage crisis. The CIA in particular thought a Reagan-Bush presidency would be in their best interest. After all, Reagan's campaign manager, William Casey, was ex-military intelligence and the would-be Vice-president George Bush had led the CIA a few years earlier. Also, the Carter Administration had come into office in the years following former President Richard Nixon's abuses with a pledge to clean up the agency. Shortly after becoming president, Carter cut the numbers of active CIA by two-thirds. Many in intelligence felt burned by Carter and were eager to see him ousted. They saw their opportunity in Iran. The Republican Party had a great many connections in the international intelligence field, and some thought that this would be a good time to use those connections.

The mission, spearheaded by William Casey, sought to make certain that Carter would not gain politically from a release of the hostages before the 1980 election: an *October Surprise*, as Casey's team called it. Even though none of the Reagan staff were actually in government at the time, they were able to use complex networks of former and current intelligence officers to help gain inside information on Carter's efforts to free the hostages. Closer to the election, the Reagan-Bush campaign held secret meetings in Europe with Iranian emissaries and spelled out their position: If the Iranians waited until after the election to free the hostages, Reagan would make it worth their while.

Meanwhile, tensions between Iraq and Iran were simmering. Iraqi President Saddam Hussein was concerned that Shiite Muslim Iran was trying to spread its Islamic revolution to the majority Shiite population of Iraq. Further escalating tensions, an Iranian had attempted to assassinate Tariq Aziz, a close friend of Hussein's and deputy prime minister of Iraq. Iraq-Iran border skirmishes were on the rise. Feeling that Iran was in a weak position militarily, Hussein decided to use the somewhat chaotic situation in Iran to his advantage. The revolutionary Iranian government was going through its own purges of "counter-revolutionaries" (leftists, mostly) in its assertion of the Ayatollah's theocracy. Many of the top officers in Iran's military who hadn't fled were either in prison or dead; leaving Iran in a poor position to defend itself from an invasion.

Seeing an opportunity to stop the spread of the Islamic Revolution and protect his regime, Hussein launched a pre-emptive strike into Iran. He felt the war would be over in a matter of months. It lasted eight years.

Iran had plenty of military aircraft and munitions, mostly purchased from the U.S. while the Shah was in power. Their main problem was a shortage of trained military officers and a lack of spare parts. After Iran was attacked, officials in the new Iranian government lobbied to free most of the military officers and use them to defend Iran against Iraq. This helped to solve half of Iran's military problems. However, the issue of finding spare parts for the Iranian military fleet wasn't as easy to resolve. It may have been easy to get high-tech military equipment on the black market, but the Iranians found it nearly impossible to get routine items such as ball bearings and tires through those same channels.

This is where William Casey and the CIA entered the picture.

William Casey was a military intelligence officer during the Second World War and good friend of Ronald Reagan, who asked Casey to manage his 1980 campaign and eventually head the CIA. It has long been alleged that Casey and his CIA connections spent a great deal of time behind the scenes making secret deals with Iran to provide the spare parts it needed in the war against Iraq. To do this, the Reagan-Bush team exploited Iranian animosity toward the Carter Administration. The case was made that there was little hope that arms could be shipped to the Iranians under a Carter presidency because of hard feelings over the hostages. Under a Republican regime, however, such shipments could and would be made through third-party countries. These third parties were necessary since Carter had imposed an arms embargo on Iran.

Essential to Reagan-Bush team's plan was an agreement that Iran would hold the hostages until the election. The Reagan-Bush campaign knew that if Carter were to pull off an *October Surprise*— a release of the U.S. hostages at the last minute— it would be nearly impossible to de-

feat Carter. This was the greatest threat to Reagan and his followers' ambitions. It was crucial to ensure that the hostages were not harmed, but also not released, until November 1980.

The Reagan-Bush campaign allegedly worked covertly to orchestrate a favorable resolution of the hostage crisis. Carter desperately tried to free the hostages, but failed in his efforts. When the 1980 election took place, the hostage crisis became the main issue and eventually cost Carter his presidency.

To further humiliate the president who had given temporary safe-haven to the Shah and refused to send him back to Iran for trial, the Iranians held the hostages for the remaining days of Carter's presidency even after the election resulted in a Reagan-Bush win.

On January 19th, President Carter announced "an agreement with Iran will result, I believe, in the freedom of our American hostages." The response from the Reagan camp, the day before Reagan was to be inaugurated: "This administration will not negotiate with barbarians or terrorists."

Moments after Ronald Wilson Reagan was sworn in as the 40th president of the United States, the revolutionary government of Iran gave the official announcement that the 52 remaining U.S. hostages would be freed. The former hostages immediately boarded a jet in Tehran bound for America.

To date, controversy lingers over this series of events. The Reagan Administration has always denied any collusion with the Ayatollah before Reagan took office. However, former Iranian president Abolhassan Beni-Sadr and Reagan campaign manager Barbara Honegger both claimed that these secret negotiations did occur, and hold those claims to this day.

While evidence about the *October Surprise* plot is inconclusive, future events made the scenario that much more plausible. Certainly, it foreshadows the trail of deception that came to be known as the Iran-Contra Scandal.

Grandpa

Front Porch Interview

Twenty-eight years ago in a small oil-patch town in south Texas an anonymous railroad crane operator, known to us as Grandpa, achieved a personal goal that very likely also set a record in the invisible world of boxcar graffiti. Marking his tag on freight trains had been a life-long habit beginning when he was a child in the early 1920s. 60 years later, after his retirement from Hughes Tool, boxcar drawing became a full-blown obsession. On January 1, 1980, he began to keep a daily record of the number of railcars he marked with his signature graffiti—a simple line drawing of a blank staring face below an infinity-shaped hat with the name BOZO TEXINO squarely lettered below it. By December 31 he had, in that one year alone, decorated 30,358 rail cars with the Bozo Texino logo. An estimate of his lifetime total conceivably exceeds 350,000 drawings.

As a kid, Grandpa's father—also a crane operator—pointed out the name Bozo Texino chalked on freight cars. Bozo was a common nickname at the turn of the century, not unlike Bubba in the 1970s or Dude in the 1990s. History is unclear as to whether the name Bozo Texino was already in use as a tag then, or if a Mr. J. H. McKinley, an engineer from Laredo, invented the Texino surname when he created a fancy cowboy sketch to accompany it. In either case, by the age of five or six, young Grandpa had seen Mr. Mac's drawing, and began fiercely copying it onto any and all freight cars he could get to. Grandpa claims his father had built him a pair of stilts to help him reach the sides of the cars. Meanwhile in Laredo, McKinley was taking heat from his employer, the Missouri Pacific, for marking on their cars. It seems that even though McKinley only drew on non-MoPac rolling stock, MoPac cars kept rolling in from Houston with Bozo Texino drawings on them. It turned out Grandpa, like any young writer, was hitting anything that rolled with his copy of Mr. Mac's dude. Word came down to Grandpa's father to have that kid quit marking MoPac cars with Mac's drawing. Grandpa, a determined and maturing young artist, said screw that. So he developed his own version of Bozo Texino—his being more streamlined, faster, and using less chalk. Thus Grandpa was able to establish his own character, increase his output, and keep hitting any car regardless of company.

The following conversation took place at Grandpa and Grandma's house in 1992.

Who is Bozo Texino, is that you?

No, it's just a drawing. Talkin' about these, I'm talkin' about the ones that's marked on one side—I don't ever count them. I count the ones that's marked on both sides of the car.

So that number, 30,000 drawings in one year, that's actual cars marked, not drawings?

Yeah, cars. Yeah.

That's right. If I didn't get it on both sides I didn't count it. To me it used to be if you marked a car it's on both sides. So, you know, maybe mine's a little different than a lot of 'em. But you know, it's kinda unbalanced just on one side. I wanted to see that people at both sides of the crossing could see it. It's silly, but that's just one of my quirks, I guess.

60,000 drawings in one year, that's got to make you the top boxcar artist.

Aw, naw. I'll just say this: as far as the number of cars marked, I don't think too many of them would ever tie me.

What do you think people think when they see Bozo Texino?

I don't know. It's kinda confusin'. I guess like on mine, if you see a big hat, why, you'd kinda think cowboy, then whenever you'd read the name, uh, I'm sure there weren't too many cowhands with that kind of a name. But I guess the main thing I thought about was that people would see it. "Where did it come from?" They don't nobody care where it's goin', but "Where did it come from? Where were they when they put this on?" I'll say a big percentage of 'em says, "I wonder why that damn fool spends time doing that when he could be doin' something else?" It's silly to some people. I'm sure at different times people wonder, "Who, who marks that?" And then they'll wonder why, and all that crap. Maybe I'm lookin' on the wrong side of it, but, uh, they'd be right, why would a so-and-so waste that much time doin' it? So you got to get enjoyment out of it or you ain't going to do it.

New Haven, CT, 1996 *by Dana Mozer*

What did your co-workers think of it?

They'd just see you doin' it. They didn't make no big deal out of it. But you know, it didn't appeal to most people.

People didn't think you were strange?

I don't believe I ever had anybody kid me about it. You know if they did I would have busted their damn jaw. But anyway, I never heard from somebody that said something to somebody about it.

What made you draw so many Bozo Texinos?

I got a pleasure out of puttin' on there and I hoped people got a pleasure out of seein' it go by. To me the picture and the name has no earthly meaning. It was just a kind of picture, like I said, one I enjoyed and I hoped other people enjoyed. It has no meaning whatsoever. It means nothing. ▰▰◆

FIG. 15.—FLOATING TRAP

In August of 2002, I ended a four-year break from fishing and returned to Kodiak to work for my sister's new boyfriend. Eric had a big fancy boat and needed someone to skiff and stack leads for the last couple weeks of the salmon season. My housemate and I flew north from Portland, Oregon for a working vacation.

The first night out on the *Northern Light* we threw the hook and went to sleep in Macdonald's Lagoon up in Izhut Bay, like I had done at least once every August for nine years. When I crawled into the bunk in the dark fo'c'sle, I was overwhelmed with a strange feeling of déjà vu—except that I knew that I had been here before, doing the very same thing. I felt timeless, like I had woken up on the *Northern Light* after a very long and realistic dream where I had quit fishing, moved to Portland and bought a house with a bunch of people. A doom settled on me in that narrow bunk in the dark, a suspicion that I was fated to repeat the banalities of the deckhand's life over and over. I could almost hear the laughing of the sea gods to whom I owed my life, whom I had not until now realized that I served.

Well, I guess there are worse things than being someone who needs to run away to sea every once in a while.

August in Kodiak is a slow, boring grind out on the grounds, and it's rare for anyone in the fleet to have anything new to share. The excitement of June red fishing has long since worn

away, any scandals arising from the island's various Fourth of July parties have been run through the gossip mill too many times to provide even the feeblest entertainment and the huge pink hits of early August are already two weeks past. Nobody has any fireworks left and even alcohol is a tiresome bother to most, not worth the inevitable hangover.

It is customary for boats to approach each other while they engage in salmon fishing. Skippers regularly exchange information about what the tide is doing or where a particular snag might be. Often, what begins as a casual inquiry will develop into a thirty-minute visit, as bored skippers glean new topics of amusement from the picked-over August menu. I've heard long radio exchanges detailing a week's worth of dinners, how they were prepared and what was on the grocery list. I've heard skippers discuss the dreams their deckhands had the night before.

So it was with some small delight that Eric reintroduced me to the fleet during the particular intellectual void that is August. I'd stand out on the bow as Eric drove up on this or that familiar face, some skipper in a ball cap and sunglasses with a summer beard who squinted quizzically at our approach before he finally recognized me as I leaned on the anchor drum, smirking, my arms across my chest. "Well, look what the cat dragged back," this or that guy would say, "I thought you were gone for good." There would ensue a little catching up, not too detailed, before we bid our farewells and hunted up another boat.

The best part was watching the big, involuntary smiles break across the faces of the fishermen. Eric grinned too, under his stubble and ball cap, happy to be the bearer of good news, or at least of a prodigal deckhand returned to the grounds after a long absence.

I seemed to be the only good news that summer. I was shocked at the size of the fleet. In 1998 I left behind a fleet 300 strong. In 2002, there were barely a hundred boats fishing, I was told. For as many fishermen as I greeted, there were those who had packed up and sold out of the fishery.

When I asked my friends and fleetmates

37

how things were going for them, the broad smiles vanished. My pals on the *Libra* were blunt. The skiffman, a close friend of the skipper's who fished every summer without fail and managed genuine friendliness on even the longest, most miserable fishing days, surprised me with his bitterness. "I regret every cent those canneries are making off of us this summer," he said, "I haven't felt good about fishing once this whole summer, because I can't stand making them money. It makes me sick." The stern of his skiff read *Vanishing Breed*, printed in black tape.

In early spring, some changes on Cannery Row drastically affected the fleet. Processing giant Ocean Beauty Seafoods acquired Cook Inlet Processors; Kodiak Salmon Packers closed down altogether. This left 70% of the fleet dependent on one big foreign-owned processor. The remaining fleet was spread out over three other canneries.

The season started off with a strike. The Kodiak fishermen, represented by the United Salmon Association, had been negotiating preseason contracts with the processors since their triumphant stand down of 1997, but this summer, the processors had flatly refused to deal. USA membership voted to stand down. They set up a co-op fishery with a small processor who cooperated with USA negotiating terms. Fishermen stood together long enough to organize tender service for boats allotted to participate in the co-op fishery.

Then Fish and Game announced a fishing period on the Mainland.

The Mainland is notorious in the Kodiak fleet. It refers to an area on the Alaska Peninsula across from Kodiak separated by the sometimes-treacherous waters of Shelikof Strait. It takes most boats about four hours to make the trip in nice weather. If a storm blows up, boats fishing the Mainland can be stuck for at least a day, possibly two or three, while the wind screams up and down the strait.

One of the worst weather days I ever fished was on the Mainland. The wind went from a steady 20 knots to a gale force 50 during the hour it took us to set the net and bring it back.

In the skiff, I pushed the throttle of my little outboard all the way down for what seemed like forever as the crew struggled to bring the seine aboard. I fought against the wind that threatened to blow the entire operation onto the inhospitable shore, as the gap between us and the vicious-looking rocks grew steadily smaller. When we had finally hauled the last of our 250 fathoms of net back and hooked up the skiff, we faced a harrowing ride to an anchorage around a tiny cape. All hands stood by on the top house. We watched our net almost float off the back deck a couple of times after we took a few big waves while we tried to turn the corner.

The anchorage was small, crowded and had a terrible bottom. We spent the next 15 hours engaged in miserable anchor drills, setting and resetting the hook every half hour or so as the wind blew us steadily off our kelp-ridden purchase on the ocean floor. We lost almost three days of fishing—half a day to the storm, a day on anchor and a day returning to Kodiak. It was an expensive gamble for us.

But the Mainland has a strong red run, which is a temptation many fishermen cannot ignore. The Mainland promise of high profits and high poundage always stirs up the fleet.

During the 2002 stand down, a substantial group of boats headed across the Shelikof for the opening. USA and the cooperative processor worked out some kind of deal for a tender to service the Mainland fleet, so guys could fish and continue to participate in the strike. But something went wrong. A storm came up, and the delayed co-op tender got stuck in town. Across the Shelikof, USA boats had fish on board with no sanctioned tender to collect them. The big processors had sent tenders over to mill among the striking fleet; they anticipated a breakdown in the complicated co-op fishery and were poised to take advantage of it. They broadcast steadily that they were available to take fish from anyone, anytime.

Guys tried to hold out, I heard, but it was too much for some. The thought of ruining a load of expensive, hard-to-catch reds by either waiting for the co-op tender to arrive, or by beating back across the strait in the storm was more than they could bear.

The first guy to cross the line was a prominent fence sitter who had made several vehement arguments against the 1997 strike. When guys saw him deliver, there was a stampede of scabs, while other guys stood by and watched. This effectively ended the resistance; within a few days USA issued a press release directing fishermen to resume individual negotiations with their processors.

By the time I showed up the bitterness expressed by the fishermen had calcified into despair. Several scabs were pointed out to me. When I asked about the proceedings, the negotiations, guys gave short, flat answers. "What negotiations?" one guy said. "They squashed us. That's the story."

One day I followed the strikebreaker scab down the dock. I offered him a copy of my zine and asked about his part in the stand down. He was very polite. He shook my hand, gave me a ten-dollar bill as a "donation," then excused himself. He invited me to call him as he hurried away. That was the only time I saw him during my three-week visit, and I never did get through on the phone.

But I didn't try all that hard, either. People were so flattened; I didn't have the heart to pick at wounds so fresh everyone still seemed to be licking them.

I did collect a few stories on a tape I then promptly lost, so what I have of the story are my memories of the fleet in defeat. I was around to witness at least two uncomfortable, 'Well, guess I'll be going now' farewells from fishermen who had made the tough decision to sell out that fall. It was sad.

I went to dinner at a friend's and the subject of the strike came up. My friend's wife, who didn't fish, was angry and full of argument. She had plenty to say about the whole business, including how we could fix it. She gave us an earful fit to crack the hearts of the hardest processors, but her husband and his longtime crewman sat quiet and grim. "What are you gonna do?" her husband finally said, and echoed a fleetwide sentiment, "We lost. They won."

ELEVEN

"Can you see what that sign says? I don't even know where the fuck we are. I hate house shows in bumfuck Egypt." Katlyn said while she was driving us to a show on the northeast end of Miami. It was a quarter to midnight and we passed a 24 hour mini-mart in a Haitian neighborhood. A man walked down the sidewalk and peered through the windows of the car. Katlyn hunched and swerved the car around him to take the next left turn.

"Don't hurt me, I'm just a helpless little white girl." Katlyn said to herself.

"Should we feel sorry for you?" I said to her, with cynicism.

"I'm just saying. I don't wanna get shot."

"Don't you think violence in places with lots of poor people who aren't white comes from whitey busting on their neighborhoods? You best be getting why some dude from here's gonna sneer at a white kid in a nice ass car." From the back seat, I turned to Eddy, who was sitting beside me. "Why did we get a ride with this girl anyway? She's making me wanna rip on punk kids and it's making me feel self-deprecating."

"You know your knack for invincibility always comes back to you. You'll forget her once you get home and write Yami a letter about riot grrrl and butt sex."

"I told you, invincibility isn't my goal- getting over self-hate is."

"Self-love can make you pretty invincible."

"But shit happens, you know? Self-love can break. Then you gotta learn how to love yourself all over again."

Every morning I would wake up and play "Hey Suburbia", the Screeching Weasel song. It was my power suit. Ideally, songs would give me power- songs would provide me with the vigor and strength I sought. Not speed, not co-dependency, not good masturbation- just a two minute song. But after two minutes, I'd recall the truth of how that invincibility wanes.

We would drive seventy-five on the freeway because that's how fast Julian's car could go. The resurgent appeal of growing up fast would consume us, and I'd yell something obscene out the window. That year, it was what any self-respecting Cuban girl would do- and my knees were allowed to be dirty this time. However, that spring, I broke one time. After the joyride and before the breakdown, I sat on the curb and talked about Selene, distinctly for the last time.

"Is this what our bodies are for? For getting manipulated and fucked over?" I asked Marietta.

"Why do you say that?"

"I heard Selene dropped out of school cause she got raped by some senior. I can't fucking understand why someone would think its okay to be selfish enough to rape."

Marietta embraced me, but I could only keep questioning the ideas we had talked about a year ago on my bed. How self defeating is it to develop your sexual confidence and have it torn by some dude who couldn't shove his dick someplace else? We built on our esteem for years. We created towering boundaries and defenses, we became fierce; and then the piercing incision of rape destroys sixteen years of teenage toil.

"We work on ourselves so fucking hard and then they fucking break us." I told her. "I can't fucking deal."

This was new to me. It was the first time rape had ever crossed my mind or even my language. It was the first time I reminisced and digressed over all the bouts of sexism that tortured me in the past. All their insults, all their attempts at coercion, and all their attempts at tarnishing the relationship between me and my own body. At the time, I had never been raped; but the normalization of sex as an act of control existed before me for the first time.

Selene was seventeen that year, and it was the last I had seen of her. I spent time alone every day- pacing on ninety-degree concrete, trying to sing to myself, sweating. I questioned why we didn't have this power to adore our bodies and have our inhibitions, our gestures, and our ability to say no mean something valuable. I questioned why no didn't mean anything to the kid who always asked me to fuck him after fourth period. Because "no" meant "please ask me again to suck your dick during music class". "No" meant silence. I wished I could tell Selene that "no" meant something to me; and even if I couldn't stop rape, I would try to give her bouts of power. I would be her two minute song.

41

consent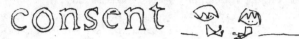

One really important way to be supportive is to make sure that you, yourself, aren't doing things that may be abusive.

A few years ago, me and *andrea* put together this list of questions about consent. Not all of the questions have right or wrong answers. We put them together with the hopes that it would help people to think deeply, and to help open up conversations about consent.

I know it's a long list, but please read and think honestly about these question, one at a time.

1. How do you define consent?
2. Have you ever talked about consent with your partner(s) or friends
3. Do you know people, or have you been with people who define consent differently than you do?
4. Have you ever been unsure about whether or not the person you were being sexual with wanted to be doing what you were doing? Did you talk about it? Did you ignore it in hopes that it would change? Did you continue what you were doing because it was pleasurable to you and you didn't want to deal with what the other person was experiencing? Did you continue because you didn't want to second-guess the other person? Did you continue because you felt it was your duty? How do you feel about the choices you made?
5. Do you think it is the other person's responsibility to say something if they aren't into what you're doing?
6. How might someone express that what is happening is not ok?
7. Do you look only for verbal signs or are there other signs?
8. Do you think it is possible to misinterpret silence for consent?
9. Have you ever asked someone what kinds of signs you should look for if they have a hard time verbalizing when something feels wrong?
10. Do you only ask about these kinds of things if you are in a serious relationship or do you feel comfortable talking in casual situations too?
11. Do you think talking ruins the mood?
12. Do you think consent can be erotic?
13. Do you think about people's abuse histories?

14. Do you check in as things progress or do you assume the original consent means everything is ok?
15. If you achieve consent once, do you assume it's always ok after that?
16. If someone consents to one thing, do you assume everything else is ok or do you ask before touching in different ways or taking things to more intense levels?
17. Are you resentful of people who want or need to talk about being abuse? Why?
18. Are you usually attracted to people who fit the traditional standard of beauty as seen in the united states?
19. Do you pursue friendship with people because you want to be with them, and then give up on the friendship if that person isn't interested in you sexually?
20. Do you pursue someone sexually even after they have said they just want to be friends?
21. Do you assume that if someone is affectionate they are probably sexually interested in you?
22. Do you think about affection, sexuality and boundaries? Do you talk about these issues with people? If so, do you talk about them only when you want to be sexual with someone or do you talk about them because you think it is important and you genuinely want to know?

23. Are you clear about your own intentions?
24. Have you ever tried to talk someone into doing something they showed hesitancy about?
25. Do you think hesitancy is a form of flirting?
26. Are you aware that in some instances it is not?
27. Have you ever thought someone's actions were flirtatious when that wasn't actually the message they wanted to get across?
28. Do you think that if someone is promiscuous that makes it ok to objectify them, or talk about them in ways you normally wouldn't?
29. If someone is promiscuous, do you think it's less important to get consent?
30. Do you think that if someone dresses in a certain way it makes it ok to objectify them?
31. If someone dresses a certain way do you think it means that they want your sexual attention or approval?
32. Do you understand that there are many other reasons, that have nothing to do with you, that a person might want to dress or act in a way that you might find sex?
33. Do you think it's your responsibility or role to overcome another person's hesitancy by pressuring them or making light of it?
34. Have you ever tried asking someone what they're feeling? If so, did you listen to them and respect them?
35. Do you think sex is a game?
36. Do you ever try to get yourself into situations that give you an excuse for touching someone you think would say no if you asked? i.e., dancing, getting really drunk around them, falling asleep next to.
37. Do you make people feel "unfun" or "unliberated" if they don't want to try certain sexual things?

38. Do you think there are ways you act that might make someone feel that way even if it's not what you're trying to do?
39. Do you ever try and make bargains? i.e. "If you let me _____, I'll do _____ for you"?
40. Have you used jealousy as a means of control?
41. Have you made your partner(s) stop hanging out with certain friends, or limit their social interactions in general because of jealousy or insecurity?
42. Do you feel like being in a relationship with someone means that they have an obligation to have sex with you?
43. What if they want to abstain from sex for a week? A month? A year?
44. Do you whine or threaten if you're not having the amount of sex or the kind of sex that you want?
45. Do you think it's ok to initiate something sexual with someone who's sleeping?
46. What if the person is your partner?
47. Do you think it's important to talk with them about it when they're awake first?
48. Do you ever look at how you interact with people or how you treat people, positive or negative, and where that comes from/where you learned it?
49. Do you behave differently when you've been drinking?
50. What are positive aspects of drinking for you? What are negative aspects?
51. Have you been sexual with people when you were drunk or when they were drunk? Have you ever felt uncomfortable or embarrassed about it the next day? Has the person you were with ever acted weird to you afterward?
52. Do you seek consent the same way when you are drunk as when you're sober?
53. Do you think is important to talk the next day with the person you've been sexual with if there has been drinking involved? If not, is it because it's uncomfortable or because you think something might have happened that shouldn't have? Or is it because you think that's just the way things go?
54. Do you think people need to take things more lightly?
55. Do you think these questions are repressivve and people who look critically at their sexual histories and their current behavior are uptight and should be more "liberated"?
56. Do you think liberation might be different for different people?

There are barometers for what we are capable of. Rachel says people can always work harder and I think she would work in her sleep if she could.

In Seattle, there was a vegan café owned and mostly run by an older man named Robin. He woke early and baked pastries and biscuits. If they ran out of jam or apples, he would shuffle up the hill to the grocery store, then return to serve huge slices of cake with coffee. My friend Eric owned a café in another part of town. He said that it that if Robin could get up every morning to bake again, then so could he. And so our little vegan bakery kept going.

Paul and Helen were like that. I thought that if they could decide to move back to town, after their house flooded, and Paul had to give up the clinic, then I could keep my shifts at the bike shop. They returned exactly one year after they evacuated. There was "Great Flood" commemoration march. Paul and Helen carried Francis Pop, not yet 2, with a sign pinned to his back that said "New Orleans Native". Helen made post card projects to mark the one year passing of the storm. They were pictures of their flooded house, after the water went down, with a form letter on the back stating that your artwork/bicycle/book you might have had in their house was lost/beyond repair/damaged. It was a charming card about loss and stuff, celebrating the artwork their friends had given to them and we all still had. If we can't smile about these small losses, how can we move on?

When I saw Paul and Helen at the march, I was sweaty and overwhelmed, but grateful for every friend who was still in town. Helen said they had just rented a house near mine, that we were nearly neighbors. Their house in mid-city still needed a lot of work before they could move back in.

44

Two months later, at Francis' 2nd birthday party, their temporary living room was filled with toddlers and play-dough and vegan cupcakes. Friends arrived with birds for Francis, drawings and small toys, as Helen requested when she invited us a few days before. It was grey outside and their house was white walled and drab compared to the bright colors of their home in mid-city.

A few years ago I interviewed Dr. Paul for a zine on radical health care. He is an MD, Canadian, anarchist vegan who can write you a prescription for anti-biotics and refer you to an acupuncturist. As I interviewed him, Rosie the pig snorted through my bag looking for the cookies at the bottom. Helen cooked carrots for Francis' first taste of them and interjected

bits to Paul's stories. I asked Paul why he stayed in New Orleans, which was a common inquiry even before the hurricane. Homicides were reported nearly every other day and many friends of mine had been held up at gunpoint. Paul said he wanted to be useful, that this city needed so much. We could take our skills elsewhere and live an easier life but here the impact and need is obvious. He also told me he loves the weather, the people, and that Helen wanted to close to her family in South Carolina.

They invited me to stay for dinner, which included rice and vegetables and two kinds of vegan cookies. They were patient with my questions and fumbling tape recorder. I rode home content with our talk, the same questions in my mind I asked him, why do we stay?

Helen and Paul's decision to move back with Francis surprised me. But it was also so good to see them here, among other friends who had stuck it out through the post-hurricane summer. If only we could always be this strong, feel as safe and sure in our convictions. A friend recently described his own outlook as optimistic, maybe idealistic, in that if we work hard enough following what we believe to be good, things will turn out ok for us.

Helen's death broke that in me. It made me angry. It still feels terrible and ridiculous and impossible to be true to say that someone entered their house, shot them, and Helen died.

That night, friends gathered at different houses, including ours. Thea cooked dinner, and people arrived, sitting in the kitchen, the front stairs, sometimes talking about what to do next, sometimes sitting silent, and holding each other. I didn't talk. I was still too angry, too hurt. For the next week, every time I thought about it, my chest filled with fluttering sudden violence. I didn't want to hurt anyone but I wanted to get the rage out. Smash things until the anger was gone. I read the newspaper stories about it—Helen's death was maybe the 12th in a week in the city. The story read like a nightmare and I hated the sensationalization of it and the truth at the base of it. A week before, Dinerral Shavers, a drummer for a local brass band, The Hot 8, was killed, shot in his car. Someone told me about it Christmas day. He is the second member of the Hot 8 to be killed in four years. I remember when their trombone player, Shotgun Joe was killed by the police as he allegedly was driving a stolen vehicle.

There has been a city-wide response not just to Helen's death, but Dinneral's and so many others who have been killed. The murder rate makes New Orleans, at least for that week, one of the most dangerous cities in the world. Some people demand more cops, believe in arming themselves for safety. There is an obvious root to the problem, if no simple solution. There is a lack of resources in this city, of social services and funding for schools. There are few jobs that pay well, even if you went to school, and not a lot of opportunity for anything better. There is an obvious disparity between rich and poor, leaving many people needing to look out for themselves however they must. People are desperate and disconnected and do not see a way out. Certainly the government offers no encouragement. Police harass people in the streets in the name of crime prevention, and claim they cannot get co-operation when they need it. However, when my neighbor witnessed a shooting on our block, the police, when they finally arrived, did not question him. A few days later, police returned to that house and arrested three women. One of my students from bike class lives there. There are so many reasons to be angry and frustrated. It is easier to not care.

Helen would've had a loving response to this. She would have found light in this situation. Jason called me from Los Angeles a week afterwards as he was on his way to plant a tree for Helen. I met him at an Easter party at Paul and Helen's, as they announced that Helen was pregnant. On the phone, Jason and I talked about Helen's good spirit and love. This is a conversation I've had with many of my friends. Writing about the tragic death of loved ones sounds heroic and memorials always sound flatly fantastic. But no one would argue these truths about Helen. Maybe this is what I am supposed to learn. But I find it difficult to find any good in this when Helen's death was against everything her life embodied.

A few days before her death, I made a resolution to approach situations with more love and less anger. I have been so tired, so worn down that I expect the worst even from my friends. The anger and frustration is self-perpetuating. My anger was embittering me, justified or not. How do I continue to believe in the possibility of good in this with its anger and disconnection, when I had to call John G. and tell him from 2,500 miles away that we shouldn't give up?

ONE OF THE GUYS?

Over the weeks, my friendship grew with the local leadership grew, but I found myself harboring confusing mixed opinions of the guys. Soon after arriving I noticed what a genuinely friendly, polite man John was. One day a couple of lawyers from the International arrived to help with some legal dispute and John offered them something to drink. When one asked if he had any bottled water, he said, "Sure. Hold on a second," and disappeared, only to show up three minutes later, huffing, bottle in hand, after having jogged three blocks to a convenience store. Just as he was winning my heart with that kind of southern hospitality, he would nonchalantly make some racist comment like, "Damn that Tiger Woods. Can't *they* at least let us have one sport?" Tim was the same way. One day he spoke really passionately and poetically about how much he cared about the union and how proud he was to be helping his co-workers improve their situations. But then a few minutes later he asked, "Hey, Andy, when's Melinda coming back? She sure has a nice set of tits on her, doesn't she?!"

In general, the gender politics around the office were a little Twilight Zone-ish. On most occasions the only woman in the building besides Melinda was Connie. Connie looked to be in her late 50s, but had bleach blonde hair and played the part of a ditzy teenager. She couldn't seem to figure out how to run the copy machine or use Microsoft Excel and spent much of the morning arranging donuts and coffee on a table and then sitting around flirting with the men. The guys flirted back and often referred to her and Melinda as "girls". I could hear the announcer saying, "You're entering a strange world where feminism never happened!" Despite the hyper-masculine atmosphere, the kind of unwitting homoerotic horseplay that commonly crops up in sports teams was prominently on display too. Of the guys I met

at Linden Hall, I quickly decided Bill was my favorite. He was the most progressive of the officers—a genuinely sweet, concerned guy, who not only served as the union's treasurer, but was also active in the local Democratic Party. He also turned out to be the friskiest of the bunch—smacking other men on the butt and performing his patented trick of putting his arm on a guy's shoulder, then reaching over and sticking his tongue in the man's ear! So weird. One week I mentioned that I was planning to take a weekend trip out to St. Louis to visit my girlfriend. All the guys did the usual, "Aw, shit! Someone's gonna get some action!" schtick. But Bill took it a step further. When I got out of the car the next Monday, he said, "Woo, boy! You must be whipped! I bet you've got nothing but ground chuck down there, eh?" and proceeded scoop down and grab my D!

47

Responding to the racism, sexism, and homophobia was a delicate and tricky matter. I felt it was important to challenge those attitudes, but it was also important not to drive a huge wedge into our team at the same time. I usually tried to say things like, "Saying things like that is not helpful to our work." It was really instructive for me because over and over I was faced with precise moments where I could benefit from white privilege, male privilege, or straight (seeming) privilege, by getting in on the joke or being one of the guys. Tim had wanted to bond with me over oogling Melinda's breasts. John welcomed me, the weird young punk, as part of a white *us*, as defined against a Black *them*. Some times I reacted to these challenges better than at others. Sometimes a grunt of disapproval or a poker face was all I could muster.

Melinda's fears during the training turned out to be somewhat founded, but not entirely. Some days the local officers seemed eager to dig in to the campaign, but at other times people would disappear for days on end and it felt like Melinda and I were pulling teeth to get anyone to help us with critical tasks. I watched on numerous occasions as guys sat around for hours watching the tickers on Headli News to see how their stocks were doing. The irony of th bowled me over—I can't think of a better example of vided class interests—but didn't seem to phase them. Th put me in the strange position—having a little more org nizing experience, but way less steel making, union, a life experience than these men 30 years older than me— of trying to be the taskmaster. Somehow in the mix, a mutual respect began to congeal.

Some of the guys hanging around the union hall had a funny way of interacting with me. One day fairly early on, Dan asked if I had ever shot a gun before. I admitted that I hadn't. "Aw, you've got to come out to the rifle range and shoot with me sometime while you're here!" he exclaimed. "Uh…okay," I answered. "As long as I don't have to shoot any animals." "Animals? Naw, just targets, " Dan assured me. "We'll bring my M-16 out there. I just got a Russian assault rifle you can try out if you want." I wasn't dying to play RAMBO with some high powered automatic rifles, but I'm always up for a new experience, so I just reiterated, "Okay. As long as we're not shooting anything living." A couple days later another guy who had overheard the conversation asked, "Hey kid, did you go out shooting yet?" When I said I hadn't, he started laying in to Dan. "The kid's begging to go shooting! Take him out there! He's just waiting to go shooting!" No one ever ended up taking me shooting, but a similar conversation happened again a couple weeks later, this time with the Health and Safety Officer. "Kid, you ever tried moonshine?" "Can't say I have." "You're in Kentucky! You've got to try moonshine." "Okay, yeah. I'd try some moonshine." A couple days later someone checked up on me, "Did ya get any moonshine yet?" "Nope. Not yet," I said casually. "Get this kid some moonshine!" the guy bellowed. "He's dying to try some moonshine!" But no one ever brought me any moonshine either.

The picnics, according to the plan we had developed at Linden Hall, were intended to build-up to a large public march and rally which we would hold a few days before the contract expired. Local 1843 hadn't had a rally or march in decades, so no one had much of a sense of how many people would turn out and how things would go. On the day of the event people trickled into the union hall slowly throughout the early afternoon, but half an hour before the march the place was packed and people were spilling out all over the lawn. Getting people lined up and starting to march took some effort, but the cops had blocked off a lane of traffic for us, and we sprawled out over three city blocks. I was just about the only one chanting as we marched, but Ashland hadn't seen anything like this in years, so thousands of people in the street, even without making a lot of noise, made quite an impression. Finally, I felt like all the time I had spent typing and photocopying and having meetings had a really physical manifestation that might actually help the negotiations.

As time got down to the wire, with only a few days until the old contract expired, the bargaining team was meeting with the company almost constantly. Though we had certainly sparked renewed interest in the union, we didn't exactly have a well organized and militant army ready to strike should the negotiations fall apart. Though we started making tentative plans for the day after, all parties involved we're crossing their fingers for a last minute settlement. For the sake of everyone working at the mill, I hoped the negotiators could reach a decent deal, but I also had somewhat selfish motives. The day after the old contract expired, my friend Theo was holding his annual Labor Day weekend campout party, Tickstock, at the farm he rented outside of Little Rock. I really wanted to go. Really really badly. So badly, in fact, that I had my roommates Q and 2:00 am when we got a call from the hotel, where the negotiations were taken place: we had a deal! People started to go nuts. The negotiators got back from the hotel, and everyone packed into the union hall's main room. Tim went over the details of the contract—we hadn't drilled them the promised asshole, but we had done pretty good. People generally saw the new contract as a victory for the Steelworkers. Everyone who was left at that hour was ecstatic, giving hugs and handshakes all around. Many people thanked Melinda and I for the help, which felt great. I went to bed thinking, "We won the first campaign I worked on! I'm going to go party for three days!!!'

Deanna, Q, and I arrived at the farm early the next morning and people were still waking up as we walked in. One of the first things I saw was a girl wearing a homemade jumper with little dangling balls around the hemline and a patch of a pirate with pigtails on it. She looked at me with incredible dark brown eyes radiating out from behind a confounded mess of curly brown hair, and smiled, revealing two of the biggest dimples I'd ever seen in my life. A mutual friend introduced her as Kim, and my heart fell out on the floor and started wiggling around like a spastic puppy.

Over the next couple days it became clear that Kim also had a spastic puppy heart that wanted to play with mine. Unfortunately, we were both dating other people at the time. A rather dramatic and difficult couple months followed, which I don't believe any of the involved parties would care to have recounted in detail here. Suffice it to say that it was an entirely new situation for me and I didn't handle it perfectly. May the riddle on the next page serve as not only as an a brief intermission to this seemingly endless (though, I'm sure you will agree, *fascinating*) glimpse into the world of union life, but also as an overdue self-reproachment for some mistakes I made in the course of falling hard for a girl with a smiling bumble bee tattooed on her upper arm.

I had first read about vasectomies, learned about the process involved and its benefits to other forms of contraception when I was 19. I was really intrigued. It was in Punk Planet Magazine, I think. A vasectomy is a surgery that involves cutting off the pipelines in your body that put sperm in your ejaculate. Basically it causes you to be sterile by closing off the proper plumbing. At that point I knew that I never wanted to have biological children and if I ever did have kids I would want to adopt and make a firm decision, knowing that I was ready to have a child. As a result, I knew that a vasectomy was something I was interested in and would seriously consider, however I had never had surgery before and was very squeamish where pain might be involved.

50

But this was serious. Did I want to turn into one of my friends with another accidental child that would convert my life to something less than the grand plans that I had laid out for myself? Hell no!

It took me until I was 25 years old but I finally worked my shit out and called around to get information locally about vasectomies. Well, actually Alex ended up getting most of the information from Planned Parenthood for me. Without that I probably would have put it off for another year or so. She was really into the idea as well and we talked about the benefits and how it would affect our relationship.

I had to go in for an interview and consultation about the surgery and meet with a doctor who would confirm that I understood it was permanent and that I shouldn't plan on a reversal or storing semen. If I thought I would ever remarry and want to have kids I should reconsider the surgery. The interview cost me 75 dollars and I didn't feel like I learned anything or did much, other than convince the woman that I had been pretty committed to this idea for 5 or 6 years.

I then made an appointment to go back and get the surgery done. There was a painstaking wait for 2 months while I watched the date get closer and closer and dreaded the pain that might be involved.

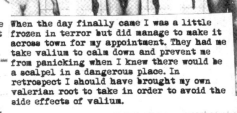

When the day finally came I was a little frozen in terror but did manage to make it across town for my appointment. They had me take valium to calm down and prevent me from panicking when I knew there would be a scalpel in a dangerous place. In retrospect I should have brought my own valerian root to take in order to avoid the side effects of valium.

There are two kinds of vasectomies. One involves a single incision and a laser that cuts through each tube. It is much less painful with a quicker recovery but it is much more common that your body fixes itself with this method. For that reason, Planned Parenthood opted to use the alternate version which involves two

scalpel incisions, one in each testicle. They sever the vas deferens, cauterize the ends, and tie them into knots. You also need stitches with this method but it has a much higher success rate and your body is very unlikely to fix itself.

I sat down, prepared myself, and sat there in wait. It didn't seem like the valium was doing anything at first but I think that is because it's effect is to make you calm, not drugged - especially calm in the rare moment that people are poking sharp instruments into a sensitive part of your body. The surgery was really pretty easy considering all that was involved. I made jokes, asking the nurse if Christians came in to get vasectomies as a form of birth control. I thought it was funny but she wasn't amused and it turns out her family was Christian. The whole deal took about 2o minutes and I was back on my feet holding an icepack to my testicles and waddling back to the lobby.

I went home and sat on the couch for a few hours before going to bed. I slept for most of the weekend, waiting for the swelling to go down so I could begin to lead a normal life again. We had some Canadian house guests at the time and one of them was motivated enough to go and get a vasectomy of his own. That makes me feel like I'm succeeding at doing vasectomy outreach and education on some minute, personal level.

THE MAN, THE MYTH, THE LEGEND

THE RISE

60TH ANNIVERSARY
THE PICTURES

50 YEARS OF
SI PHOTOGRAPHY

The plot thickens

ENEMY
OF THE STATE

Oppression Breeds Respect

FROM THE
ASHES
AID's warrior

When the Prison Gates Are Opened, the True Dragon Will Fly Out!

I began a friendship with Nadel. I considered him and his daughter my family. John helped me get ahold of both players and I invited them to my event. John would slip me numbers for athletes and I would interview them. I would ask them to speak to Nadel and he would get a scoop. I was able to hear in his voice one day how sad Nadel was. I asked him what the problem was and he informed me that his daughter was using a new drug called "meth" or "ice". Over the next few years I would call his daughter and talk truthful about how drugs ruin you and you never know till you're through! I was told that I made a difference one day when I was contacted by Fox Television who wanted to do a special on me and Stacy! I saw this girl turn her life around and graduate college!

After being in some of this country's most violent prisons I had to check myself every morning when the guards and inmates would say "good morning". I would ponder why they were being so nice and what they wanted. I was floored one day when I saw on ESPN that Len Bias and Don Rogers, two young athletes had died before their lives had really begun. I had a vision to start a program that would help young athletes from the inner city to deal with this drug epidemic. I loved working with Stacy Nadel and talking to kids that were in trouble. Boxers Against Drugs (BAD) was officially created that evening. I called my attorney for advice and direction. I met with Warden Luster and in three weeks presented a list of visitors for this boxing exhibition that began with Boom Boom Mancini and ended with three pages of the who's who in the sports and entertainment world. Eric Davis and Darryl Strawberry would drop in on fight night. I had to hire a secretary because I could not keep up with requests from parents and celebrities who sought my help. I thought of Carlos Palomino and called Mr. Nadel, who ran a story on Carlos and I. The story went on the wire and I blew up; the phone ringing and ringing.

I called Mr. Palomino and asked if he remembered a young kid asking for a shot at his title named Joey Torrey. He laughed and I told him my situation and that I wanted him to come to my promotion at the prison to help me with this BAD program. Carlos was there the day of my first promotion. Miguel Diaz would bring in five boxers - one I was following was Antifoshi from Nigeria. He was on his way to a title shot. In one month from this day in Jean, NV, this young kid Antifoshi would fight for the title and be dead from punches suffered in that battle. Top Rank would bury him, send a body bag full of silver to his family, and then move on to the next victim!

From that prison hell and creating BAD I reached many children in the next decade with their sports heros reinforcing the power of family and staying in school. My main goal was to let these kids know that they could do anything without using drugs. This message would be seen worldwide on television shows. I needed to fund the vision and my first business venture was using my art talent and creating a portrait of Darryl Strawberry in his batting stance with the NY skyscrapers at his waist and the traffic of Broadway St running through his feet as he hit the NY apple. I called his mom and we created a t-shirt for her church to sell. I made my first six figures by selling the art work and rights to a watch company. I would call Daryl and Eric at their homes or hotels. I owed this new beginning to them. I would call Darryl on Long Island and we would talk the morning of home games. His brother Ronnie was going through drug problems and I reached out to him. Darryl was partying and lost but did not realize it yet; money will buy you time. For the next three years Darryl and Eric would co-sign me with other players and I would call Kevin Mitchell in San Francisco and ask for Mike Sadek, the old catcher for the Giants and tell him that I need to get ahold of Kevin. Once connected, I would tell Kevin that Straw, and "E" are my boys and I need him to sign ten dozen baseballs for me! Ana Luisa would buy baseballs at $60 per dozen. Once Mitchell would sign the ball I would have them pre-sold to collectors for $2,000 per dozen! I did this everyday – five, ten players per week! It was 1986, the hottest time in history for sports memoribilia. Then it branched out to Eric Davis calling me when he would be on a road trip in Atlanta and ask me to get a break away back board put in his backyard. I would call Reebok and they would pay for it. Eric and other players need their cars driven down to Florida for spring training. I would make everything happen.

In 1998 I was once again called to the warden's office. There sat my father looking old and beaten. His clothes were hanging on his body as if they belonged to someone else. The warden stood up, touched my shoulder, and said "Sorry" as he walked out and closed the door behind him. My father looked down and said that both he and my mother had cancer. I sat there numbly as he went on - he had lung cancer and my mom had cancer of the blood. He told me about the Anaheim fight and many others - he thought I would lose and wanted me to lose. I looked at him confused and he said "You were the fighter that I could never be and a father should not be jealous of his own son, but I was." He started to cry and I took this frail man and felt his pain. I realized children are not born bad and it's not in the blood. A child is a product of how he is brought up.

I moved him to Vegas and took care of him. I had baseball players call him, mail him signed bats and balls, and even had Darryl and Eric invite him to a Dodgers game – in the dugout! John Nadel would call my dad and invite him to other games. Angie from the forum club would invite him to fights. My mother was in the hospital with a rare blood disorder. I spoke to the doctor who gave her three or four days to live. I called Carlos Palomino and together we called California Department of Corrections. I asked for the director, Jim Gomez, and was connected with his secretary. I told him "I am in another state for saving the life of a correctional officer and I want a chance to kiss my mother before she passes." He told me to hang up and Carlos got to talk to Jim Gomez. I tried calling them for hours to find out anything. I finally got to talk to Mr. Gomez and he told me "I am letting you go free for the day but if you run I will hunt you down!" I had my agent transfer money to pay for the bond to leave.

I found out later that this journey was unique; based on a law that stated "no convicted murderer will be released into society for any reason." I drove down to LA with Carlos. We arrived and hospital security told me that if we needed help with the convict their office was down the hall. I told them it was ok and I had it covered.

I saw my mother all hooked up to machines then ran to the waiting room for shots of tequila. She was in a coma and I would ask her to look out for Dolly and Blanca and spent hours telling her about Ana Luisa, who had sent her flowers on Mother's Day. I left and tried to call Ana but every time I put a dime in the phone and dialed, it just came back – until Carlos told me it was 35 cents now.

I drove back to prison and found out the following day that my mother had passed away. I drank a fifth, smoked a joint, and got back to a new venture producing the TV show *Rapamania*. I was called for an attorney visit with Steve Shiffman, Carlos, and Harold Lipton, the father of Peggy Lipton from the *Mod Squad*. They asked me to come in and help promote the show which would air on pay per view around the world – split screen between Apollo Theatre and Hollywood Bowl. It would be the country's top hip hop artists and they wanted me to get the artists for a 33% cut. I started my phone day by calling Eric Davis or his cousin Renard Young, a former UNLV football player. I

MR. G. & JOEY

JOEY & EMMITT SMITH

would call Dion Sanders and tell him when his leather was ready and then ask him to sign thirty jerseys. I made a million in 1988 and spent it all on clothes for kids I did not know!

I invented myself again, finding a way from a prison cell to contact these ball players. I would grab the Las Vegas Review Journal and go to the baseball section and the road games. If the Reds were in New York I would call the Mets public relations department and inform them that I represented Eric and needed his hotel number. I called Eric and asked him to tell Bobby Bonilla that I would be calling. Eric would collect all the broken bats and equipment he could gather and leave it at the front desk. I would have FedEx pick it up the next day to send to a baseball shop that I had sold it to that morning. I talked to players in the jacuzzi, playing cards, or the visitor's locker room. I got calls from players like Jeff Bagwell, Bobby Bo, and others who needed cars moved, tickets obtained, or jewelry bought.

I was taking bets from Pete Rose, who would bet with the bookie, who in turn would send the money that I would turn over to Sacco with Pete's bets. This fool never bet on baseball and never won. Pete was the Reds' coach at this time and I would get calls from players for hotel rooms, shows, etc.

It was the holidays of 1988 and Carlos Palomino was working a boxing event as a commentator when he was asked about me and what I was managing from the prison cell. The following week all hell would break loose as I was featured on the George Michael Sports Machine, Fox Television, The Reporters, and A Current Affair. The word was out and I started to be handed bags of mail. I was introduced to a program called Youth Development, Inc in Albuquerque - a model of what a national program should be – working with gang kids, finding jobs, educating, and housing single mothers. I spent the next few years helping those kids with director Chris Baca, a very educated man who became my mentor. I met his assistant Ron Chavez, who took me in.

I was paying $3,000 per month in phone bills. I would call Japan to get Eric and Darryl card show appearances, call players daily for bats and balls, and call my dad to make his day. My dad would say things like "Guess who called me today? Bobby Bonilla."

I would get my morning messages ranging from Edward James Olmos wanting me to read his script, to the family sweating me for money, to Brian McRae needing bats and balls for his big brothers and big sisters program. I was making so much money and sending 200 kids to Magic Mountain, sending bikes to a Christmas program, and hiring an appeals attorney, Cheryl Lutz. Melvin Belli was trying to obtain me a governor's pardon from Pete Wilson. It was going well until Belli went

on a media blitz saying that Pete Wilson should be put into the bay on a boat without paddles. I began to read law in the evening as I mapped out the following day.

I remember one day Eric Davis told me "You get'n large," - during Spring training he hit a single and while stopped at first base, Jeff Bagwell asked him "How's Joey?"

The off season was spent connecting players to card shows. They could make ten grand in two hours and would donate the money to me. I would send back eight grand and this way they didn't have to report it. Rapamania was a hit and I was able to get Ice Cube, The Lynch Mob, and Debbie Allen as the MC. Stevie Ray Vaughn visited me but I did not know who he was. I was musically at the other end.

Around this time my dad told me that Paul Molitor of the Baseball Hall of Fame was Puerto Rican. I called coach Sparky Anderson who gave me the right number. He had seen the Sports Machine featuring me and I told him he was a great Puerto Rican. He said he was French Canadian while holding back laughter. Fuck'n Papi!

A lot of players tend to let me coach them off drugs and then forget about me and refuse to talk later. The players from the 'hood though, they never forget me. Eric, when interviewed during my roughest times, said "Joey is my friend."

After thinking about it for a few weeks I decided I wanted a transfer to New Mexico and attempted it. I was doing big things with YDI and had nothing holding me back. It was 1990 and I had my visiting form approved for Carlos, Alexis Arguello, and a man named Milch. Carlos and Alexis both visited me the following Saturday. I greeted Alexis warmly, as he is the one of the greatest fighters to ever lace the gloves on, and he introduced me to David Milch, who I had found out was Sacco's biggest customer and made Pete Rose look like a kid. He was spending 6 figures each week on bets. He also produced and wrote Hill Street Blues, NYPD Blue, and Tombstone. He was interested in telling my story as an ex-junkie from Brooklyn, himself.

Carlos told me that I was approved for transfer to New Mexico and good luck. I hung up and went to Mr Sacco and explained my situation. I owed him fifty large but we laughed about it and he let it go. I sent a donation every week to the Gambino lawyer. Things were done for me in return. When Mr. Lipton did not want to pay me for Rapamania, he was visited along with Quincy Jones and his ex-son-in-law. Paul Shiffman said "You're in prison. Come and get it." Mr. G made them see Jesus and I was given a hundred grand of the million collected. When you have nothing, you have nothing to lose.

ON SUBBING: THE NEXT FOUR YEARS

It's been almost four years since On Subbing was first published in book form. I deliberately wrote it without a big conclusion, no final point to tie everything together neatly because this isn't the end. There's something fatalistic about reducing a large chunk of your life to a series of words to begin with. To then put a cap on it, a full stop and treat it as a complete unit that's over now, a dead piece of your past to be shelved away and brought out only for purposes of nostalgia; that's just plain ridiculous. I wasn't going to stop subbing, and I didn't want my book to imply that.

The funny thing is, shortly after the book came out, I did stop subbing. About a month into my fifth year with the district I accepted a permanent position. I decided to go for it for a couple reasons. First, a lawyer from the special education office had found a couple issues of my zines. We had a brief, very unpleasant meeting wherein she first calmly pressured me to stop writing for legal reasons, then tore into me personally, calling me a bad sub and saying it seemed like I didn't enjoy working with the kids. The bad sub part hurt. Maybe I wasn't good at my job, I don't know. But the second part, it didn't seem like I enjoyed working with the kids? That was just asinine. I'm not the most competent writer, but I know my excitement and joy in working with the students I have is evident in my zines and book. After another five minutes of haranguing me and telling me how bad I was at my job, how I need to be trained, and how I should probably look for other work because I obviously don't respect the students, our meeting was over. And she ended the meeting by saying, and I'm being totally honest, "You know you always get good reviews from the teachers you work with." As she was walking me to the door she asked, "What are you doing this weekend?", all chummy like. I don't know, you wanna have a sleepover? You could slam my head in your car door a few times then we could do each other's hair.

So I thought taking the permanent position would give me some job security. And I also felt I was ready to move on. I felt as though in four years I had seen all the kinds of classes and learned about as much as I was going to learn from subbing and I wanted the challenge of staying in one place.

Gaining a deeper understanding of my students and building on their strengths and interests, figuring out how to become a good, consistent disciplinarian.

And this ended up being my ideal job. I worked one-on-one with a special needs student in a mainstream kindergarten class. I liked the set-up of the school. There were pods instead of classrooms, with three to four foot high bookshelves separating the classes. It could get a little hectic and noisy at times, but there was much more interaction and sharing between classes. The staff was supportive and friendly. I liked the teacher I worked with, though she wasn't very good at keeping order. But that was good because it forced me to step up and be the disciplinarian for the whole class frequently, and in turn I figured out how to do it without getting into silly power games. (That's not to say I *never* fell into silly power games.)

But the best part about the job, of course, was my student. He was such a sweet, smart, funny kid. He was wary at first and kept his distance, usually hiding under a table, but he warmed up to me. And when he did we worked very well together. The work I did with that student and the achievements — both academic and social — I helped him to reach are without a doubt the proudest accomplishment of my life. I deciphered his speech, which was a little English, a little Spanish, but mostly mumbles. I helped him work on his

verbal skills by playing with robots, his favorite things.

How cool of a job is that? We'd make Lego robots, they'd battle a bit, mine would give in, then they'd have a conversation.

I also got adept at interpreting his expressions. That look meant he could do the work but was being difficult, and I knew to stay on him. However, a similar look meant he was getting over stimulated and was about to blow out. That's when I'd take him out of the class and walk him around the school. We'd say hi to the secretary and librarian, check out the bug collection by the amphitheater, if the weather was nice we'd go out to look at my bike and I'd let him try on my helmet. Then we'd head back to class, ready to work.

By the end of the year he was interacting with his peers appropriately (and the rest of the class were such sweethearts they always included him in free time and group activities without having to be asked) and had far surpassed the academic goals set forth in his Individualized Education Program. Everyone at the school was pleased with the work I did with my student, and like I said, I'd never felt more satisfied or proud. And it broke my heart that I couldn't continue working with him the following year.

There were actually three separate and insurmountable reasons why I couldn't keep what felt like a job tailor-made for me. First, due to the budget cuts, I got laid off. The district needed to drop some employees and the most recent hires were the first to go. My paperwork wasn't finalized until January. I didn't stand a chance. There was a chance I could overcome that. The staff liked me and the principal said he'd fight to keep me on. But it was a moot point. The administration decided to un-mainstream my student and put him in a special ed. first grade class. No one-on-one assistant would be needed. No one at the school thought that was a good idea, but nothing could be done. But that was a moot point as well, his family was moving out of state. The bottom line, I had absolutely no hope of carrying on.

This was one incident in a string of bad luck that chased me out of Portland. There was also the bike accident where I t-boned a car and suffered a fractured clavicle and scapula. The scapula is the triangular kind of bone behind your shoulder. Apparently those don't break very often.

I heard my doctor bragging about it to someone in the hall, "The guy in here has a fractured scapula!" That laid me up for almost a month.

Then there was my prolonged, severe illness. I developed Crohn's Disease. I've written about it elsewhere so I won't go into great detail here, but it lasted three months, one of those being the most miserable, terrifying month of my life.

Then, after a sweet, carefree month of traveling, I come back to Portland only to get hit by a car again. This time there was no real damage to myself or my bike, but it seemed a clear sign that Portland didn't want me anymore. So my Dad came out to Portland, we loaded up his car, and I headed out to Philadelphia, a fat check in my pocket from the settlement of my first accident, ready to set me up in my new home.

I have some dear friends in Philadelphia and I fear that there's no way they're not going to be upset with what I'm about to say, but moving to Philadelphia will go down as the biggest mistake of my life. It turns out Portland was just pulling my pigtails and knocking my books off my desk. Philadelphia *really* hated me. I've never experienced such raw hostility from every direction. The air was abuzz with a menacing hum and people were just waiting for any excuse to kick someone's ass. An ice cream truck driver cut me off while I was biking, stopped and then stared me down for no apparent reason. Shortly after I arrived I went to the bank

and opened an account, my blank checks were sent to my neighbors, who promptly wrote checks to their friends and cleared out my account. A huge sinkhole developed in the street in front of my house and after hearing countless cars bang into it, I decided to put a traffic cone next to it. And just for a laugh, I put this four foot teddy bear I'd found the previous night into the sinkhole. A neighbor saw me and accused me of being racist; that the bear was an effigy of a black man. He was really upset and I thought, "Wow, here I am at 31, about to get my ass kicked on my own front porch for playing with a stuffed animal."

My teaching experience was very limited in Philadelphia. It's probably a good thing, because Philadelphia has some notoriously rough schools. I heard a high school teacher got his neck broken over a confiscated iPod. And according to the story, he was a well-liked teacher. What would happen to an odd, little beardo like myself? I worked two days a week, two and a half hours a day, teaching an after school program. I started with fifth graders and there was an instant, very open enmity in the class. It was pretty miserable. After a couple weeks they shuffled the classes and I got four second graders. It was better, but not much. I was not at all upset when that job ended.

The only other job I had in Philadelphia was a one week, temp job tearing down a display at a museum. It was one of those old punk hand-me-down jobs. When the museum needed extra hands, like when tearing down or setting up the displays, the one punk who worked there permanently would call his friends.

Money was really tight after that and I decided to get food stamps.
I was biking up 54th Street and next thing I know I'm waking up in an ambulance. A couple high school kids knocked my bike out from under me and started kicking furiously. I only knew that because the paramedics told me. I ended up with a broken jaw and a fracture in my frontal sinus bone. I know you can't keep running from your problems, but screw it. Philadelphia is dead to me and the University hospital can suck that $10, 000 bill. I left a month later.

Right now I'm in Kansas City, and I work as a para-professional in a Montessori school. It's a change from regular schools and it has taken me a while to get the hang of it. The teacher gives lessons to small groups and the rest of the class is expected to be self-motivated enough to find work until it's their turn for a lesson. It seems like the role of the para is to stay back as much as you can, only offer help if asked or if a student is having trouble finding work to do. I like my class, twenty-one 3-5 year olds, and they've given me some funny stories, mostly scatological. But I'll keep those to myself, partly because I don't want to end the book with a series of shit jokes, but mostly because I don't want to go overboard with it. I don't want to relate every interesting experience I have teaching until there's not a scintilla of excitement left in what I write. Besides, now that I've stopped subbing and started taking permanent positions, I guess I'm interested in the bigger picture now.

57

Skipper

Steve and Heidi's Authentic Creole Tofu and Rice

Music: Eyehategod-In the Name of Suffering lp (1992)

1 onion, chopped
2 green peppers, chopped
Several cloves garlic, minced
1 couple stalks celery, chopped
Olive oil
2 cups water
Sea salt
Pepper
2 lb extra firm tofu, cubed
Nutritional yeast
Soy sauce
2 Tbsp roux (see below)
Hot sauce
½ little can tomato paste
Basil
Oregano
Thyme
Cayenne pepper
Cajun seasoning (see recipe this book)
As much rice as you'd like

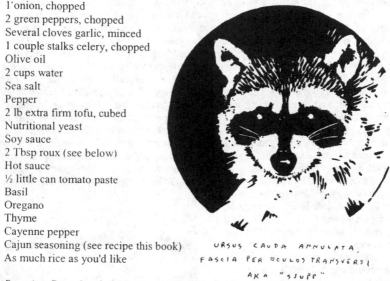

URSUS CAUDA ANNULATA,
FASCIA PER OCULOS TRANSVERSI
AKA "SJUPP"

Roux is a Deep South thickener which can be made as such: Put whatever amount of margarine you want into a saucepan and melt. Add in an equal amount of flour. Stir quickly. The resulting mixture should be doughy in consistency and amber in color. Apparently it becomes a more effective, more flavorful thickener the longer it cooks. Keep refrigerated.

Preheat the oven to 350°F.

Fill the bottom of a small bowl with soy sauce and fill the bottom of another bowl with nutritional yeast. Coat each of the tofu cubes with soy sauce, then with nutritional yeast. Place each cube on a lightly oiled oven tray and cook in the oven for 20 minutes or so.

Next, get the rice going. This will probably take 20 minutes or so as well. In a small pot, boil the 2 cups water. Add the tomato paste, roux, and hot sauce to taste. Reduce to a simmer.

In a large pan or wok, stir fry the onion, peppers, celery, and garlic in a bit of olive oil. Add the salt, pepper, basil, oregano, thyme, and cayenne to taste. Mix the roux/tomato sauce into the stir fried vegetables. Mix in the baked tofu as well. Serve over the rice with Cajun seasoning and extra hot sauce.

Sweet Potato Burritos

Music: Ingurgitating Oblivion-Voyage Towards Abhorrence lp (2005)

3 tsp vegetable oil
1 large onion, chopped
4 cloves garlic, minced
6 cups cooked kidney beans, rinsed and drained
2 cups water
3 Tbsp chili powder
2 tsp ground cumin
4 tsp prepared mustard
Pinch cayenne pepper
3 Tbsp soy sauce
4 cups cooked and mashed sweet potatoes
12 (10 inch) flour tortillas, warmed

Preheat oven to 350° F.
Heat oil in a medium skillet. Saute onion and garlic until soft. Add the beans and mash. Gradually stir in the water and heat until warm. Remove from the heat and stir in the chili powder, cumin, mustard, cayenne pepper, and soy sauce. Divide bean mixture and mashed sweet potatoes evenly between the warm flour tortillas. Fold up tortillas burrito style. Bake for about 12 minutes.

Cheeseburger Macaroni

Music: Stiny Plamenu-Ve Spine Je Pravda lp (2001)

3 ½ cups macaroni (uncooked)
½ cup vegan margarine
½ cup flour
3 ½ cups boiling water
1 ½ tsp salt
2 Tbsp soy sauce
1 ½ tsp garlic powder
A pinch of tumeric
¼ cup oil
1 cup nutritional yeast
Paprika
1 package fake hamburger (Morning Star crumbles, etc.)

Cook macaroni and set aside. In a saucepan, melt margarine over low heat. Beat in flour with a whisk, continue to beat over medium flame until mixture is smooth and bubbly. Whip in boiling water, salt, soy sauce, garlic powder, and turmeric. Beat well to dissolve the flour mixture. The sauce should cook until it thickens and bubbles. Whip in oil and nutritional yeast.
Heat fake hamburger in a frying pan. Mix part of the sauce with the noodles, put in a casserole dish. Pour a generous amount of sauce on top and mix together. Mix in fake hamburger. Sprinkle with paprika. Bake 15 minutes in at 350° F oven. Serve.

THIS SUMMER, LIKE MOST, WAS HOT... REALLY, REALLY HOT. WITH THE HEAT OF THE SEASON CAME THE OH SO FAMILIAR BUGS OF SUMMER. THERE WERE THE BUGS THAT WE DIDN'T MIND SO MUCH (MAYBE EVEN ENJOYED) LIKE JUNEBUGS AND CRICKETS. UNFORTUNATELY THERE WERE ALSO THE TORMENTORS - FLEAS, MOSQUITOS, AND FLIES. THIS SUMMER, EVERY NEW PIECE OF PRODUCE BROUGHT INTO OUR HOUSE SEEMED TO BE A SACCHARIN MATING CALL TO ONE PARTICULARLY ANNOYING BREED - THE FRUIT FLY. THESE THINGS WERE SUCH PROLIFIC BREEDERS, THAT A WEEK OF NEGLECT OF OUR OWN PERSONAL POPULATION WOULD ENSURE THE INFILTRATION OF THESE BUZZING BOTHERS IN EVERY CRANNY OF OUR SPACIOUS PAD - NOT JUST THE KITCHEN, BUT THE BATHROOM AND BEDROOMS AS WELL. NOT ONLY DID THEY GROSS US OUT, BUT IT WAS HARD TO PASS THEM OFF AS PETS WHEN WE ENTERTAINED, "HERE'S YOUR BEER, PAL, BUT LET ME FISH THAT FLY OUT FOR YOU FIRST." DETERMINED TO MINIMIZE THE PRESENCE OF THE FLYING MOOCHERS IN OUR HOUSEHOLD, I DID SOME RESEARCH, AND COMPILED SOME INFO ON HOW TO TRAP, KILL, OR DETER THE PESTS. I SPENT A COUPLE WEEKS PUTTING EACH METHOD TO THE TEST SO THAT I COULD SHARE WITH YOU THE RESULTS OF MY EXPERIMENTS ON

HOW TO GET RID OF FRUIT FLIES

THE MOST IMPORTANT THING TO DO IS TO FIGURE OUT WHERE THEY ARE COMING FROM (WHERE THEY ARE MAKIN' BABIES). MY FLIES WERE VERY ELUSIVE - I NEVER REALLY FOUND EVIDENCE OF ONE DISTINCT FLY HATCHING EPICENTER, BUT I DID THE FOLLOWING THINGS TO SORT OF COVER ALL THE BASES.

① Check to see if they are coming from a sink drain. Fruit flies need a source of moisture and food to reproduce - this makes a seldomly used sink drain the perfect place. To check this possibility,

You can put plastic wrap over the drain pipe and tape it down. Wait a day or so to see if little flies appear trapped under the plastic. If so, this might be the fly nursery. Scrub the inside of the drain if possible or rinse it with a blast of high pressure water if you have a spray nozzle fixture on your sink. You can also slowly pour boiling water down the sides of the drain to dislodge any larvae. YUCK! Once done, remember to use the offending drain more often—getting water to run through it more regularly will prevent the flies from settling in.

② Look for maggots (tiny rice looking things that wiggle) in wet caulking around your sink or tub. Clean these areas and dry them thoroughly. Check any wet dishtowels or sponges. If they might be a nesting site – boil them and let them dry. Look for any drips under the sink or behind the fridge that might be creating a suitable breeding climate for flies and remedy these types of problems.

③ Take out your trash more frequently Flies love to linger and breed in the soupy mess that sometimes collects at the bottom of your trash bag. Move organic kitchen wastes outside and compost them: you will be recycling, your soil will thank you, and you will be keeping fly breeding delectables from your trash can and kitchen.

④ This might seem really obvious, but put food in the fridge. SO, of course certain types of fruits and veggies prefer to be at room temperature, but most everything can stand to be kept in the fridge, and away from the clutches of the tiny flying beast!

Those steps taken, YOU ARE READY TO BEGIN A MORE AGGRESSIVE APPROACH. FRUIT FLIES ARE FAIRLY DUMB. THAT BEING SAID, THERE ARE A NUMBER OF WAYS TO CREATIVELY TRICK ONE.

① IF you don't want to deal with catching the flies yourself, you can try a predacious plant. You can turn your animosity towards the fly into life-giving food to a curious looking plant. We have two Venus Fly Traps, one Cobra Lily, and one Purple Pitcher. There are also Sundew Plants available. All of these plants digest a trapped fly as a source of food although their methods differ. I find that ours do little in the way of reducing our fly problem because they are usually covered to control their humidity and flies can't get to them. They're pretty cool looking though! I give them a 1-fly Rating—

FEED ME

② Once, we set out a bowl of fruit and waited for the flies to settle on it. Then we got out our trusty vacuum cleaner (with a hose attachment) and simply sucked them up. You can literally suck them right out of the air. It was sort of fun. After you've collected the flies in the vacuum, you can take the vacuum outside, open the filter, and let the flies go. 3 FLIES!

③ There are a variety of sweet liquid/soap traps you can make. I set out a container filled with 1/4 cup vinegar and a drop of liquid dishsoap next to a fly-ridden area. The flies are attracted to vinegar— and the soap in the solution traps them. This trap only caught a few. I GIVE IT A ONE.

④ Similar to number 3, mix 1 cup water with a Tablespoon of Sugar and a Tablespoon of white vinegar and a drop of liquid dishsoap in a wide bowl. This trap works, but not really well.

⑤ FRUIT FLIES like Beer as much as we do. I put a dish of beer with a couple of drops of dishsoap in it on our pantry shelf and caught at least a dozen little buggers. I think they got too hammered to fly away! 2 FLIES!

⑥ Lay an almost empty bottle of some sweet alcoholic beverage (Liqueur, Guiness, wine) on its side. The bottle should have a long thin neck. The idea here is that the flies will go in but are too stupid to fly out. I found that my flies were too stupid to fly in and mostly just hung out on the lip of the bottle. a half a fly rating—

⑦ This trap is the coolest to study and by far the most effective. First you get a tall cup or jar. Put some overripe fruit in it (Bananas are good, so is jelly). Sprinkle yeast over the fruit. The yeast will help the fruit ferment and small good to the flies. Then, using paper and tape, fashion a funnel with a mouth as big as the mouth of the jar and an opening just bigger than a fly. Tape the funnel onto the jar, with the small opening on the inside. You'll be amazed how quickly this trap fills. Then you can untape the funnel outside and let them go. (or keep them and watch them make babies). FOUR FLY RATING!

CALENDAR

by Keith Rosson

DAY

Wend through streets slick with rain and darkened with exhaust. Work, eat, sleep – hours pass in an eyeblink this way. Weeks become months become years; you are continually shocked, like cold water rilled down a sleeve, confused as to where it was your youth was spent.

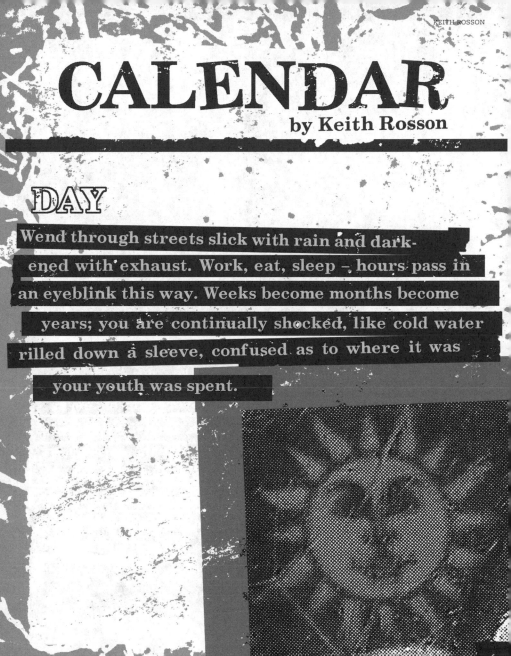

NIGHT

Measure it in cigarettes, cups of coffee, the staccato tattoo of voices on the radio. Revisit every horror, every misstep, every small and trivial error. Revisit old loves and the inevitable decay of your union. Measure your worth by the act of creation: words blackening paper, paint laid over canvas like a cowl. And even in this, in making something from nothing, this act of *bringing forth* – you are at the mercy of memories and time. Every moment a revenant come back to haunt you with its sweetness or blunt savagery.

DAY AND NIGHT

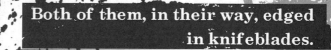

Both of them, in their way, edged in knifeblades.

MY JOB AND ANCIENT CHINESE HEALING HERBS:

At the "juice bar," (my current Food Services of America Job position) I was assigned by the corporate-esque food service manager named Mitzi, to stuff pieces of fruit and globs of concentrated orange juice into a blender to make smoothies for all the office workers of the 100 story building. I was always fascinated by the thick, ugly brown bottle of liquid ginseng that lay next to the blender at the "juice bar." The bottle looked romantically ancient and was written only in Chinese. As Mitzi would yell at us to be "team players," I would daydream that this bottle was Edgar Allen Poe's magik juice, and that only wingnutty poets and tribal sufi mystics were to drink from this bottle. Yeah, it's the team players versus the wingnutty poets. This form of imaginative thinking helped me cope with that fact that I was feeding liquid ginseng to yuppies and getting paid weak amounts of dinero, to pay rent to the drug dealing hippies.

I was tripped out on the ginseng root like wicked mad. My spacey hippie freaky roommates, more specifically Star and Randy, would munch on big chunks of ginseng root and start talking things like "the manifestation" and "the Mayan calendar splendors." They made this ginseng root seem holy especially since they always looked massively bug-eyed, like a tranced-out shaman (from this point on I thought that hippiesh folk who dumpster-dived and mooched off the government would help lead the revolution, leading us thru the concrete jungle armed with Chinese healing herbs, ready to make tea, not war.). Yet in my 18 years of existence, I had not yet sampled the root of ginseng. It was much easier writin' poetic crap and fantasizing about it.

But back in Mitzi's corporate food service land, I decided to pretend that the spirit of Edgar Allen Poe and some sufi mystic preferably named "xtallian lightin' bolt" would channel through my veins and force me to take many, many shots of the pure liquid ginseng. Much more exciting to dabble in these unknowns than the typical "run into the alley and smoke as much weed as you can" tactics that I had used to bear the froth of food service-ism. Needless to say, after a few minutes of downing the ginseng shots with the ample pace of a sorority girl taking vodka shots, a whole new realm of time space, and reality hit me. I felt as if I was living in a box and my brain and soul were mere floatation devices for a higher powers. "Mitzi, I am having a paranoia attack," I mumbled as if everybody would merely think I was stoned again. "What's wrong?" Mitzi fumed, "it's the lunch rush, goddammit."

"Mitzi, I need to sit down." I sat down on a milk crate in the back room and tried to figure out why I felt like my soul was a box, and how I couldn't seem to come up with wingnutty poetry or sufi mystik visions during this experience. Usually these people seem to have these experiences on mescaline/LSD/shrooms/etc... not ginseng! Shit damn! Was I schizo? Or the reincarnation of some force I couldn't understand? All my co workers asked what the problem was. I told them that I had drank too much concentrated ginseng extract. They all laughed. "It's only ginseng," Mitzi fumed with her subtle nazi powers. "Get back to work now!"

When people say "I am re-born!" I believe them! That's cuz I get reborn all the time, yo! Not this "it takes me 7 years to get new cells" crap. Not a bible. Not a cult. Not an identity crisis, but realizing that there is more for you to realize!! Spirlulina makes me feel like there are so many new ways to communicate with plant life! Juicing oranges, apples, and ginger root and toastin' the juice with my roommate Star helps me realize that health is way cooler than these stupid fantasies of whiskey drunk writers or tripped out ravers. I get re-born on licorice tea. (realization that tea rules!). I get re-born when I go dumpster diving (realization that you don't have to pay for stuff). I get re-born when I gather with friends and we come up with movements like "call, write, or e-mail everybody you know and tell them to call, write and e-mail everybody they know with the message: on November 3rd, 2010... let's all smile and hug each other at precisely 5pm pacific standard time! Go!"

I even get re-born on ginseng. It's easy to get re-born you know, when it's sunset and you have an awe inspiring song stuck in your head and all you do is smile at the sun melting into the sky, thinking thoughts like "whoa, dude... it's peace!" And as much as I bitch about Corporate Counterculture and the large population of humans who be all IDIOT, I really do think many thoughts like, "whoa, dude... it's peace."

EXHIBIT: A tripped out college dropout who is walking down the street, smiling, and saying "hello" to all that they pass by. The people that they pass by, not only ignore all possibility of smiling, they don't even look each other in the eye! This saddens the young, tripped out food service brat, when all they want to do is think thoughts like "whoa, dude... it's peace!"

"Yo Mitzi," I ask one morning at the juice bar, "Why is it that people seem to ignore each other when they walk down the street?" Mitzi pinched my cheeks like the corporate nazi that she was and said, condescendingly "Oh, look at you, you're sooooo cute, you're just like me when I was your age, don't worry you'll get over it." Mitzi was 27 years old as well, just like everybody in my life.

"Oh honey, you could be such a cute thing, but look at you," Mitzi said, now stuffing a Burger King breakfast sandwich into her mouth. "Honey, our boss likes to call you the little ragamuffin so maybe you could get some better fitting pants." Arrgh! This is my pet peeve numero uno! Anybody who tells me that I have to get tight clothing, thus taking away from the holy thang called COMFORT, is evil. "Mitzi, I need to have extra wide leg room comfort in order for me to properly distribute the smoothies," I sarcastically responded to the corporate food service diatribe. Mitzi stormed off to the hot dog place every time I said this. I didn't get a "20 cent raise" because the food service drones thought my pants were too "big."

Oooh, how I despised the enigma known as Mitzi. She was everything I despised about corporate lesbian-ism. She was the reason why I was scared to come out. Mitzi tucked in her corporate shirt with her pants going up almost to her neck. Mitzi also had a mullet! Why!? Why!? Why!? How many more frea-kin' lesbians must have mullets? Don't they realize that a favorite pastime of punk queers is to go mullet-watchin? I was scared that if I got enough courage to admit to the 27-year-old hippies that I was really queer, I'd automatically grow a mullet. The mullet would attack me in my sleep!

Each morning when I would chop up the pineapples and concentrated orange juice globs at the "juice bar" (and fear the wicked ginseng bottle), Mitzi would troddle her 400lb body whilst stuffin three hot dogs in her mouth. Now I don't care if Mitzi was 400lbs or not, for I am not a skinny kid myself and chunk is way beautiful, it's just that Mitzi's 400lbs were made up of hot dog fat. That's all. "You want some," Mitzi said every damn morning with food still in her mouth. I don't eat meat, I'd tell her for the gizillionith time. (My life story is about pretending to be vegan and vegetarian even though I am really just that sad kid in an animal rights tee shirt stuffing a piece of salmon into their face.) However, "meat" as a concept, was not considered a tool to help you "figure it all out" for the Urban Hermitt.

Revenge, however, was to take place. After the brutal <your pants are too big for my corporate image of fast food restaurants that call burritos "wraps"> arguments, Mitzi would assign me to the cash register at lunch instead of the juice bar as a torture tactic. "Here's two bucks" I would say when giving change. I tried to give the customers a casual experience at the cash register to keep things low stress. Mitzi didn't like this. Every time I said the word "bucks" instead of "dollars" she would march on up and make a big scene in front of the entire office worker population of The Big City... tellin' me that the word "bucks" sounded like I was an "un-educated hick" No, Mitzi... actually, that's "a do-it-yo-freakin'-self-sneak-into-college-libraries-in-theory anarchist to you, Mitzi." An Urban Hermitt does not equal an uneducated hick.

Needless to say, I soon learned a valuable life lesson: you can quit your job anytime you want! Shortly thereafter, I learned another valuable lesson: I could quit my job, but due to the powers of poverty, and that I couldn't seem to make any money selling drugs, I was forced to get another Food Services of America Wage Slave Job the following week.

Bridges

Broadway Bridge
Broadway between NW and N,
connects NW Lovejoy and N Interstate
The Broadway is a drawbridge completed in 1913. It is a double-leaf Rall type Bascule drawbridge, unique in Portland and very rare otherwise. (A bascule drawbridge is "seesaw" style, the two "draws" lift up away from each other to accommodate for riverine traffic) The Rall system uses complicated rolling lift mechanisms, meaning long delays when the bridge goes up.

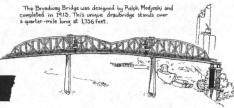

The Broadway Bridge was designed by Ralph Modjeski and completed in 1913. This unique drawbridge stands over a quarter-mile long at 1,736 feet.

BICYCLE INFO: Bicycles have bike lanes up until the bridge itself, and then are directed onto the sidewalks. The Broadway is the most popular connection for bicyclists from N/NE to downtown and the westside.

TECHNICAL INFO: Total length 1,613 ft (492m), main span 278 feet long (85m), clearance from river 70 ft (21m).
Painted "Golden Gate" Red (aka International Orange)

Burlington Northern Railroad Bridge
5.1 (aka St Johns Railroad Bridge) on the Willa-
mette River about one mile south of the St Johns
Bridge
This bridge was built in 1908 to complete the then Northern Pacific (now part of Burlington Northern Santa Fe) mainline north to Seattle. At the time it was a swing bridge, meaning that the center span would "swing" open to allow for boat traffic. Even though it was the longest swing span in the world, modern maritime needs led to the spans' obsolescence, and in 1989 the bridge was retrofitted with a vertical lift span. The twin towers can be seen for miles around.
BICYCLE INFO: No bikes!

TECHNICAL INFO: 516 ft (157m) long lift span, vertical clearance 200 ft (61m), fourth highest lift bridge in the world.

Burnside Bridge

Burnside Bridge
Burnside St
The Burnside is a bascule type drawbridge that opened in 1926. Architecturally speaking, the most significant thing about the bridge are the twin towers at each end of the movable section, done up in Italian Renaissance style. Culturally speaking, the significant things about the bridge is what goes on UNDERNEATH it. Under the westside is Portland's famed tourist trap Saturday Market, and under the eastside is the world-renowned Burnside Skatepark.
BICYCLE INFO: Bike lanes run in both directions on the bridge itself, though the connections on both ends are a bit spotty, forcing you to suddenly merge with fast-moving traffic.
TECHNICAL INFO: Total length 2,308 ft (703 m), center span 252 ft (77 m), lowered bridge 64 feet (20 m) above water

Fremont Bridge
I-405, between Pearl/Northwest and Albina
Opened in 1973, the Fremont is the youngest of Portland's Willamette River crossings. Its beautiful design is due to the Marquam (I-5) Bridge's ugliness--the Portland Art Commission was brought in to aid with design so there wouldn't be such an uproar. (We Portlanders are very particular about our bridges!) Its gentle arch (once the longest

Fremont Bridge

tied-arch bridge in the world) dominates the skyline. And peregrine falcons nest on the underside of the span. Look closely and you may see one soaring around the bridge!

BICYCLE INFO: Prohibited

TECHNICAL INFO: 2,152 ft (656m) long, main span 1,255 ft (383m) long, top of arch 381 ft (116m) above the river, clearance above river 175 ft (53m)

Hawthorne Bridge

connects SW Main/Madison on the west, SE Madison/Hawthorne on the east

Aah, the Hawthorne! This bridge is possibly Portlanders most-favorite bridge, and it's at least the city's most distinctive bridge. Many postcards feature the photogenic structure, and it can even draw big-time Hollywood directors to shoot crappy big-budget movies here (see The Hunted). Anyways...The Hawthorne Bridge is a truss bridge with a vertical lift span, and is the oldest vertical lift bridge in operation in the United States! Built in 1910, it's the city's oldest bridge but still does a lot of work. A major rehabilitation effort was undertaken in 1998-9, giving us the 10 foot wide sidewalks and green-and-red color scheme. The low clearance over the river means the drawbridge opens frequently, so it's common to be stuck waiting for the bridge.

BICYCLE INFO: The Hawthorne is the city's busiest bicycle bridge, with 1,500 bicycle crossings daily. The westside connects conveniently with Waterfront Park and the downtown grid, and the eastside connects to the Eastbank Esplanade and the Madison/Hawthorne bikelanes. Bicyclists must use the sidewalk.

TECHNICAL INFO: Total length 1,382 ft (421m), consisting of five fixed spans and one 244 ft. long

(74m) vertical lift span, clearance 49 ft (15m) above water

Morrison Bridge

between SW Washington/Alder on the west, SE Morrison/Belmont on the east

Its current version opened in 1958, the Morrison is a busy workhorse bridge spanning downtown with the Central Eastside. It's yet another Portland drawbridge, a "Chicago Style" bascule bridge (see drawing for how it opens). Built during the "we need to build a lot of stuff fast" period of bridge engineering, the Morrison is not much to look at. The "air traffic control tower" styled bridge towers (with slanted windows) are the bridge's most distinctive feature. The bridge is one of the largest mechanical structures in Oregon, due to its 940 ton (!) counterweights with 36 ft. tall gears located inside each of the piers.

BICYCLE INFO: While its central location would be great for a bicycle crossing, it really sucks to have to use a bicycle this bridge. For one, bicycles are prohibited from the roadway and must stay on the sidewalk. And using the sidewalk means using three separate series of stairs (up and down) to go around all the highway on-ramps. This sucks for pedestrians also. Sometime in the near future the Morrison will become more bicycle and pedestrian friendly, until then, use one of the other bridges instead.

TECHNICAL INFO: Total length of bridge 760 ft (232m), draw span 284 ft (87m)

Marquam Bridge

connects I-5 on both sides of the river.

Opened in 1966, the Marquam opened Portland to through driving on I-5 between BC to Mexico. The double deckered cantilever bridge sits high above the river, dominating the scenery around. The bridge itself is boring, a victim of the Vanilla School of Engineering that built the nation's Interstate Highway System, where economy of design and cost trumped aesthetics. It infuriated many Portlanders at the time of completion, and led to the Portland Art Commission helping with the design of the next freeway bridge (Fremont-1973). Great views of the city and Mt Hood abound from the bridge, for the half-a-minute commuter traf-

69

fic zips across it at least. If you're a pedestrian or bicyclist, you're out of luck (at least until Bridge-Pedal).

TECHNICAL INFO: Length of main span 440 ft (134m), length of two side spans 301 ft (92m) each, vertical clearance of the lower deck is 130 ft (40m) above the river, upper deck 15 ft (5m) above the lower

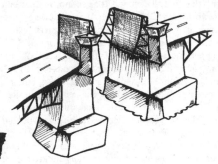

Ross Island Bridge

connects ramp nonsense on the west side, Powell Blvd (US 26) on the east

Opened in 1926, the Ross Island is named after the sandy isle in the Willamette directly to the south of the bridge. Its cantilever truss span is a subtle beauty (much like Portland itself), the more you look at it, the more you appreciate it. The Ross Island was the city's busiest bridge from its time of completion up to the opening of the Marquam Bridge.

BICYCLE INFO: The Ross Island offers remedial bicycle facilities. Bicyclists must use a narrow sidewalk and then negotiate their way around a series of off-ramps on the westside, pretty dangerous. ODOT rehabilitated the bridge a few years back, but improved the bicycle access very little, which seems to happen with all their recent bridge projects.

TECHNICAL INFO: Longest span 535 ft (163m)

Sellwood Bridge

connects SW Marquam/ Riverside on the west, SE Tacoma on the east

The Sellwood, along with the St Johns, are the least-seen Willamette River Bridges to the casual visitor, mostly due to their distance. The Sellwood Bridge is about 5 miles south of downtown, and is more useful for connecting the far-reaches of the metro area than for the city itself. The two-lane truss bridge opened in 1925, at the time the county must have thought that many lanes would suffice. Unfortunately for modern use it does not, and the bridge is overused beyond its capacity. The capacity of 32 tons was lowered to 10 in 2004 after bridge inspectors found numerous cracks in the span. Now buses and trucks can't use the bridge and the question posed is: will the Sellwood be repaired or rebuilt? Enjoy the current bridge and the great views from it while you can, because it's not going to last.

BICYCLE INFO: The Sellwood is a crucial link in the Willamette River loop, but on-bridge facilities suck. You are required to walk your bike across on the very narrow sidewalk.

TECHNICAL INFO: Total length 1,971 ft (601m) with four continuous spans, two center span length 300 ft (92m) each, two outside span length 246 ft (75m), clearance 75 ft (23m) above river

St Johns Bridge US 30 Bypass between St Johns and Linnton The St Johns bridge is Portland's only suspension bridge, and not often seen by the casual visitor (it is about six miles from downtown). Opened in 1931, at the time it was the longest suspension bridge west of Detroit (other bridges have surpassed its size since then, most notably the Golden Gate Bridge). Painted green, the bridge tends to blend in against the West Hills. It's a quite beautiful bridge and a symbol of pride for the St Johns neighborhood. The gothic arched towers and eastside support beams lent the name Cathedral Park to the greenspace and neighborhood below.

BICYCLE INFO: The St. Johns is a highly un-bikeable bridge. Bicycles must use a narrow sidewalk (after construction is done), the westside approach is steep and bicyclists must ride on a busy street. Since the bridge is a high one, going over it means making a big climb in elevation from the east. There was hope that during the current bridge work the bicycle situation would be improved, but the pleas from bicycle advocates fell on deaf ears at ODOT. Thankfully, the St Johns Bridge doesn't fulfill a vital bicycle link for in-town transit, but does come in useful for accessing Sauvie Island from the eastside.

TECHNICAL INFO: Two Gothic towers 408 ft tall (124 m), 1207 ft (368 m) center span 205 feet (62 m) above the Willamette River. Total length 2,067 feet (630 m)

goes rumbling by!

BICYCLE INFO: the top deck is remedially bikeable, though narrow sidewalks and steep approaches from the west doesn't make it that fun. Most bicycles use the bottom deck to get between downtown and Waterfront Park to the Eastbank Esplanade.

TECHNICAL INFO: through truss double lift bridge, main span 211 ft (64 m) long, lower deck 26 ft (8 m) above water, upper deck 72 ft (22 m) above water, 163 ft (50 m) of total vertical clearance when both decks are fully raised.

Steel Bridge

connects NW Everett/Glisan/Front on the west,
N Interstate/ Oregon/Multnomah on the east

The Steel Bridge is a very special bridge. It is the only double-deck vertical lift bridge with independent lift decks (the lower deck can retract into the upper deck without the upper deck moving) in THE WORLD, and the second-oldest vertical lift bridge in North America (the first being our own Hawthorne Bridge)! The Steel was built in 1912 by the Union Pacific Railroad and its primary function was as a railroad bridge, but it accommodates much more than that! It's the most diverse bridge maybe anywhere (as you'll see by the users below). Its functionality was increased with the opening of the pedestrian walkway on the lower deck in 2001, completing the downtown waterfront loop. It's quite the experience to ride your bike along the bottom deck while a freight train

"Love isn't a state of perfect
caring. It is an active noun
like struggle. To love someone
is to strive to accept that
person exactly the way he or
she is, right here and now."
                    - Fred Rogers

What I can see looks like the
setting for a shoot-out in some
cliche ridden neo-noir 16 mm
student film. The dim light
bulb doesn't have the luxury of
any covering to help dispense
of its contents properly.

Everything is so blurry at the
edges but almost in focus right
in the middle.

The hipster bar that was just
starting to be built when I
left is now finished. I
remember not wanting to look at
it on my way to work. It was
like a gruesome car accident
scene. My rational brain told
me to be respectful and just
keep going. Something deeper,
baser, and instinctual inside
couldn't keep my eyes away.

The most distinct feature was
a giant cluster of shimmering
metal squares shaped like a
camel on the far wall. It
seemed just about as out of
place as a real camel in
Greenpoint would. It just hung
there. A foreboding sinister
symbol of change giving everyone
that walked by a dirty look with
its hollow sunken eyes.

Now the whole place is done and of course, business is booming. Really though what can a bunch of old broken-down alcoholic Polish men do with a six doller shot of well whiskey? What do I do with a bartender who doesn't know what a beer-back is?

Who's space is this? In the end it seems like every neighborhood just goes to the highest bidder.

But still I miss it here so much. I miss riding the subway home alone late at night a little tipsy right before the inevitable depression hits. I miss looking out the window at the treasure chest of city lights right as the train pushes itself up from underground. I miss those few quiet times in the sea of utter madness.

I miss rat shit and big cockroaches on a freshly mopped kitchen floor. I miss hating myself most of the time and thinking I'm dirty and need to lose weight. I miss wanting to buy lots of new clothes. I miss comparing myself to the hot b-boy posters on subway platforms.

AUTOBIOGRAPHICAL DEATH

al Burian

LOGAN SQUARE, THE LAST DAYS
OF FALL .... SOON IT'LL BE TOO
COLD TO WALK AROUND AT NIGHT
WITHOUT A JACKET.

HOODIE SWEATSHIRT! STILL
WEARING 'EM! AND I'M THIRTY-
SEVEN YEARS OLD. GUESS IT'S
NOT A PHASE; LOOKS LIKE I'M
A LIFER.

ALREADY, I'M PUSHING IT --
WALKING AROUND UNDER-
DRESSED AND SHIVERING.
WHAT CAN I SAY? I'M AN
OPTIMIST!

DIDN'T I ALREADY MAKE A
COMIC ABOUT THIS WHEN I WAS
TWENTY-SEVEN? "HOODIES:"
IS IT AN INTERESTING OBSER-
VATION? WAS IT AN INTEREST-
ING OBSERVATION TEN YEARS
AGO?

"IT IS PRECISELY BECAUSE OF ALL-
AROUND CULTURAL DECLINE THAT I
SEE HOPE FOR THE COMICS INDUSTRY
TO CONTINUE," SAYS DAN CLOWES.
BUT, THEN AGAIN, FELLOW MIDDLE-
AGED HOODIE WEARER LOGAN
BAY, OVER AT QUIMBY'S BOOK-
STORE, TELLS ME: "AUTOBIO-
GRAPHICAL COMICS ARE PLAYED
OUT!"

HE'S RIGHT, YOU KNOW: OUR
LIVES ARE NOT SO PROFOUND,
EVEN IF THE DRAWINGS ARE
GOOD. STICK TO SCI-FI AND
FANTASY. FUNNER TO DRAW.

I'VE FELT "PLAYED OUT" DURING THIS LONG, BADLY-DRESSED DECADE. I WAS CRANKING AWAY AT MUSIC + WRITING, OPPORTUNITIES AND OFFERS WERE COMING IN.... IT SEEMED GREAT...

...IN ALL THAT MOMENTUM I HARDLY NOTICED THAT I WAS LOSING MY RAISON D'ETRE, MY SENSE OF WHAT I HAD WANTED TO EXPRESS IN THE FIRST PLACE.

WHAT WAS IT?

I STOPPED LIKING THE STUFF I MADE. IT SEEMED POINTLESSLY NEGATIVE. I DIDN'T LIKE THE LIFE I WAS DOCUMENTING. MY PRODUCTIVITY GROUND TO A HALT.

WHEN YOU MAKE STUFF ABOUT YOURSELF, YOU CREATE AN EVIL TWIN-A LITERARY DOPPEL-GÄNGER. WATCH OUT! IT CAN FUCK YOU UP! EVEN THE BLEAKEST ART SHOULD BE SOMEHOW LIFE-AFFIRMING. OTHERWISE, WHY BOTHER?

SO.... WHEN WE MEET UP AGAIN IN TEN YEARS, I HOPE I'LL STILL BE WEARING A HOODIE SWEAT-SHIRT, AND I HOPE THIS NEXT DECADE WILL BE DEDICATED TO... WELL... HOPE.

HERE GOES! RISING LIKE A PHOENIX FROM THE ICY EARTH OF LOGAN SQUARE!

AAAAAWK!

IS THAT DUNGEONS + DRAGONS ENOUGH FOR YA, LOGAN?

77

BUT SHE NEVER CAME

MAYBE YOU CREEPED HER OUT... JUST LIKE THIS FLYER PROBABLY WILL

CHA CHUNK

MAYBE THAT'S WHAT I WANT! SOME ONE THAT'LL LOVE ME DESPITE THE FACT I'M SEVERLY MISGUIDED! MAYBE EVEN FINDS IT ENDEARING!

So... YOU WANT ME TO HELP TEAR DOWN THE FLYERS TONIGHT? OR EARLY IN THE MORNING AFTER YOU'VE HAD TIME TO THINK?

... I REALLY FELT SHE WAS THE ONE

Sigh

(I LEFT UP MOST OF THE FLYERS ... SHE NEVER CALLED)

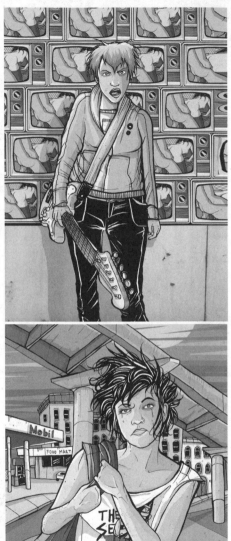

THE TOWER
GENOA, COLORADO

THEFUCKENRADTOUROFTHEWORLD

AMATEUR ARCHAEOLOGIST JERRY CHUBBUCK PULLS SOME STUFF OUT OF A DISPLAY CASE.

THE TOWER MUSEUM IS FULL OF DISPLAY CASES HEAPED WITH MYSTERY ITEMS.

"WHAT'S THIS?" HE ASKS ME IN A SOFT, SING-SONG VOICE. HE HOLDS UP SOMETHING THAT LOOKS KIND OF LIKE A KNIFE. "IS IT A KNIFE?" I ASK. "MAYBE IT'S A POLACK POTATO PEELER," HE DEADPANS. I THINK JERRY WANTS ME TO KEEP GUESSING, BUT I JUST STAND THERE, SMILING STUPIDLY. "IT'S A MAGIC TRICK," HE FINALLY SAYS. THEN HE SHOWS ME HOW IT WORKS:

① ②
STAB!

JERRY ALSO SHOWS ME:

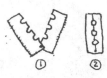

SOME WEIRD PLIERS FOR KILLING CHICKENS. OR SO HE CLAIMS.

A CIVIL WAR UNIFORM BUTTON CLAMP. THE CLAMP HOLDS THE BRASS BUTTONS STEADY SO THAT A SOLDIER COULD POLISH THEM. OR SO HE CLAIMS.

① ②

JERRY MAKES ME HOLD THIS ONE BEFORE HE TELLS ME IT'S AN INDIAN HUNTING CLUB MADE FROM AN ALASKAN WALRUS PENIS BONE.

JERRY HANDS ME A PAIR OF BINOCULARS AND I HEAD UP INTO THE TOWER. IT WAS BUILT IN 1926 BY CHARLES GREGORY ("THE P.T. BARNUM OF COLORADO"), AND FOR YEARS, IT WAS A POPULAR STOP ON HIGHWAY 24. "SEE SIX STATES!" THE HIGHWAY SIGNS PROMISED. NOW THE TOWER IS BYPASSED BY I-70 AND VISITORS AREN'T EXACTLY BREAKING DOWN THE DOORS.
UP ON THE TIPPY-TOP, WHIPPED BY THE WIND, I FEEL LIKE I'M IN THE CROW'S NEST OF SOME SHIP SAILING ON THE HIGH PLAINS INSTEAD OF THE HIGH SEAS. I DON'T KNOW IF I'M LOOKING AT SIX STATES, AND IT DOESN'T EVEN MATTER.

WHAT DOES IT ALL MEAN?

Our focus is disseminating ideas and information through the items we distribute. I want to show that zine writers and DIY artists are a credible contribution to society and should be respected as such. I feel that zines have been largely marginalized through most of their existence.

I've wanted to make literature that can be seen and understood by the general public not just an insular, elitist, segregated group of people. I think that is a large part of why many "activist" scenes fail; their focus is so insular that they don't reach out into the community. In order to make positive change we need to communicate and impact the outside world.

My ultimate goal here is connection. I want to connect with people who understand the spirit and goals of DIY ethics and fanzine culture. I want to raise awareness about the spirit of these ethics and this community to people who live in places where they have no access to it. I want to teach kids that they don't have to grow up to be lawyers or businesspersons working jobs they hate in order to pay for their cars, yachts, homes, etc. I want to find the social derelicts and teach them how to bond together to find a "family" amongst their peers. This is a bit grandiose, I know...

I want to be able to help people find meanings in their lives without using this project to inflate my own ego. This project isn't just about us, the ones behind the scenes: filling the mail orders, talking to people through letters and e-mails; it's a two way street. Send in your zines, propose your ideas, talk to us about what you are interested in, show us what you do! Tell us what we could do better. Tell us what we do well. Distribute catalogs and flyers in your town.

Microcosm provides money for a few people to live on. This is difficult terrain because it is so easy to get caught up in the fact that wealth can cause humans to forget

about their ethics and seek greater wealth. We pay ourselves from this project in order to keep it sustainable and so we can focus on being creative instead of working other jobs. It's a difficult middle ground a times. I don't feel like we would be able to accomplish all that we do if this was part time or volunteer based. The focus is on sustaining ourselves while doing something we enjoy, not making the most money possible. I feel like I've finally reached a point where I respect the work that is done here and I take myself seriously.

On the tail end of the *Cocoon: The Road Trip* tour, I was sitting on the curb in front of Needles and Pens with a very drunken and chattering Jen Starfiend while *$100 & A T-Shirt* played for a small but captivated audience perched on milk crates. A man stepped in, relatively late in the program, and emerged a few minutes later. He asked if I was the director and yelled in my face "Print is dead!". I'm not sure what he hoped to accomplish but at this point I probably couldn't disagree more....

We have a slew of new projects on our plate and no immediate end in sight. We are now scheduled to publish about a dozen titles each year.

88

singularly devoted to the sponges

"One night while rooting through the recycling bin for magazines, I found all the confidential Ph.D. applicant files for the biology department at an Ivy League university from the years 1965-1975. Stapled to many of the yellowed documents were photographs of the prospective students. They were treasures! I tore through the folders and rescued every portrait I could find. I had to have them. Only later did I realize I had to publish them".

hardly the life-of-the-party type!

DO ZINES STILL MATTER?

Some thoughts on self-publishing in the digital age

When I wrote Notes from Underground in the mid-1990s I defined zines as "the variegated voices of a subterranean world." More than a decade later, zines are still being published and my definition, I think, still holds: zines are the creative outpourings of an underground world that passes below the radar of most people.

What's surprising is how little has changed in the zine scene. Moe is still publishing her *Xtra Tuf* and still making it "free to commercial fishing women." *Cometbus* hit issue #50 and Aaron continues to tell stories about his life on the fringe, even if it's now the fringes of New York City rather than the Bay Area. Politically, zines remain on the margins of mainstream politics, staking out their position through exhortation (*Am I Mad...Or Has The Whole World Gone Crazy?????*) or expose (*The CIA Makes Science Fiction Unexciting*). And zines still revel in the absurd ephemera of our culture, be it the biographies of long forgotten, and by conventional standards quite wacky, scientists in D.B. Pedlar's *Rogue Reader*, or Chris Pernula's lovingly hand-sketched portraits of champion bowlers in *Bowling Stars of 1989* (Serious? Ironic? Does it matter?)

As evidenced by J.L. Heckman's *Work Stories*, zines still chronicle and condemn the soul-sucking labor that most of us do for money, while at the same time zines bare witness to the possibilities of a different sort of labor; work which is done, in the words of the pioneering zine scene organizer Mike Gunderloy, for "love, not money." Zines continue to champion the life of "losers" like "Bubby" in Chris Johnston's comix zine, *My Friend Bubby*. And, perhaps most important of all, zines still record and relate the everyday thoughts of maybe not so everyday people trying to make sense of their place in a world in which they often feel they don't quite fit.

Even the aesthetics of zines have not changed all that much over the past dozen or so years. Text is still cut out and pasted over images, introductions are still hand lettered, amateur pictures and comix are still scattered across pages, and the odd snippet from the mass press is still reproduced for comic or dramatic effect. From the outside many zines look the same too: photocopied and fashioned from standard size paper, folded in half and stapled at the spine. The world of zines has remained remarkably steady. Meanwhile the world of self-publishing has changed radically.

In the coda to the first edition of this book I wrote: "What is the future of zines? One word: computers." I was hardly going out on a limb with this prediction. Even back then, when the Internet had just recently broken out of its geek ghetto and the graphic interface of the Web was just beginning to take off, the transformative importance of computers to all forms of communication was obvious. Today, in the overdeveloped world at least, computers permeate nearly all aspects of our life. The price of technology has dropped, public access to the Internet has improved, and new software makes it ever easier to make and share your own media creations. We live in a digital age.

This raises some obvious questions: In this digital age, when anyone with a computer can publish whatever they want to an anonymous audience of millions, are analog zines obsolete? Are personal websites, blogs and social networking sites playing the role that zines once did? Are zines today the self-publishing equivalent of that embarrassing older guy in the non-ironic 80s-era band t-shirt who lurks at the back of rock shows? (mea culpa) To sum it up: Are print and paper zines merely an exercise in nostalgia?

In part, the answer is an uncomfortable: yes. Zine producers have historically embraced new technology. They quickly adopted small hand presses in the 1930s, mimeograph machines in the 1950s, photocopy machines in the 1980s, and desktop publishing in the 1990s – why stop now and fetishize the materiality of paper? One could plausibly argue that blogs are just ephemeral perzines, and fan sites on the web are nothing other than digitally displayed fanzines. Perhaps the only thing that separates a zine from all these new forms of computer-mediated communication is the medium.

Zines have always been more than just words or images on paper: they are the embodiment of an ethic of creativity that argues that anyone can be a creator. Professional newspapers, slick magazines, and academic journals, art galleries and television shows, regardless of their content, have a uniform message to the reader or viewer: you can't do this, you are not skilled enough, you don't have the resources, so just sit back, appreciate and consume the culture that professionals have made for you. A zine, with all its amateur, low-rent, scruffy seams showing, says something else to the reader: this is easy, you could probably create something just as good,